A Foxy Old Woman's Guide to Living With Friends

A Foxy Old Woman's Guide to Living With Friends

By Cynthia Cary

THE CROSSING PRESS
FREEDOM, CALIFORNIA

Cover design by Victoria May
Cover photo by Bonnie deJong
Interior design by Victoria May
Printed in the U.S.A.

For information on bulk purchases or group discounts for this and other Crossing Press titles, please contact our Special Sales Manager at 800/777-1048.

Visit our Web site on the Internet: www.crossingpress.com

Library of Congress Cataloging-in-Publication Data

Cary, Cynthia.
A foxy old woman's guide to living with friends / by Cynthia Cary.
p. cm. -- (Foxy old woman's guides)
Includes bibliographical references and index.
ISBN 0-89594-919-9 (pbk.)
1. Shared housing--United States. 2. Aged women--Housing--United
States. 3. Female friendship--United States. I. Title.
II. Series.
HD7287.86.U6C37 1998
363.5--dc21
98-24644
CIP

Dedicated to:
Lee, for your love & collaboration

ACKNOWLEDGMENTS

This book, like the topic it discusses, is a collaboration. Many women and men have shared their vision and experience, knowledge, skill, and support towards creating a "Crone's Nest." You know what you've given me: Kay Lambert, Ginny Gillmer, Karen Klinefelter, Nomi Green, Shelia Cowling, Laura Glicken, Karen Lyncoln, Kay Leigh Hagan, Kathleen O'Bryan, John and Helen Cary, Ann Kreilkamp, Deborah Altus, the Crone's Nest Egg, Tina Quartaroli, Maria Brenton, Barbara Conroy, Yvonne Carleton, Jo Getter, Shewolf, Julie Keene, Andrea Nedelsky, Mary Ann Hooper, Donna Davis—for all you've taught me about collaborative living; Wayne Quilico, Martha Littlebird, Linda Todd-Baca, Karen Sands, Floyd Jennings, Moon, and Barbara Hale—I'm sorry we'll never live in community together. My gratitude also goes to Elaine Gill, Jill Schettler, Cyndi Barnes and the staff at *The Crossing Press* for their support of this work.

CONTENTS

PREFACE

Once upon a time I imagined that I would grow old with my husband, spending years and years together. We would die twenty minutes apart and neither one of us would end up alone. But then, I was pretty naive.

Everything changed after my divorce. I began to wonder what my old age would be like. I didn't want to live alone—it scared me. Yet I didn't consider marrying again. And living with my stepchildren, even though I loved them, wasn't really an option. As for a retirement facility where other people would make decisions for me, where I'd become more and more passive, I couldn't accept it. So what then? I simply didn't see any decent options and I panicked.

I recalled that some years before my friend Kay told me, "When we're old women, we'll live together." The sudden memory of her casual remark became a source of comfort. I'd always felt close to my women friends, so why not live together? I could see myself clearly, sitting on a porch drinking tea with several women. I realized we could pool some of our resources to live a more satisfying life than we could singly. With this dream, I knew I could move beyond my own and society's expectations to create a desirable life as an old woman. But exactly how?

In the next few months several women told me their dreams. One friend, a single mother, visited another woman yearly in Florida in order to discuss their future together. Another envisioned a home for aging lesbians. On and on the dreams were spun—wildly varying yet similar visions of old women living together. With these ideas in mind, I became excited and inspired to go beyond my dreams to create the reality.

I struggled to find words to express my future. The word "crone" came to the surface, but not the notion of a wizened old woman; rather, a wise old woman who knows the cycles of life. She stores up the wisdom of her years, women's wisdom, and knows how to transform herself. We can choose to embrace her power. And with this, I began to change, to move more confidently toward the woman I wished to become.

As I gathered information from other women who were also seeking a solution, I began to share these ideas through a newsletter and in workshops. This became what I call the Crone's Nest Project, through which I've connected with hundreds of other women who are developing their vision of shared living or are already living collaboratively. This book is the culmination of my search. I hope it helps you realize your dreams.

INTRODUCTION

Studies show that women live longer than men, on the average about seven years. And becoming single is only a death or divorce away. We can assume that 85 percent of American women will be single in their elder years.

If you conform to society's expectations your choices are simple: live alone, with an extended family, in a retirement center, or nursing home.

If you have acquired a home, do you want to live alone there when you get old? Can you afford it? Could you manage the upkeep of the house either financially or with your own sweat?

If you have children, do you want to live with them or would they like to live with you?

What about a retirement community? Do you want to join one? Can you afford the fees? There is less expensive senior housing funded by cities, but the waiting lists are long.

Have you secretly held the nightmare of becoming a bag lady, carrying all your belongings around in a shopping cart? So many people, both women and men, are similarly frightened.

Think about it. You are 70 years old and you get the flu. Who will notice? Who will care? If you do not consciously plan for your elder years, there's a chance you will become lonely, isolated, and perhaps poor. Your protection lies in timely planning and action.

Society teaches you what your life will be like as you age. Look about you—there are few positive images of old people. How many old people do you see on TV, as prospects to buy new cars, for instance. Not many. We lack good role models. The dominant culture denies people who are old the access to resources, status, and support that it grants to youth. As we age, we become invisible; clerks and others don't see us or ignore us. Bankers and plumbers act as if we're too old to understand what they are saying. Employment opportunities disappear, complicating our already compromised financial circumstances as women.

Our society does not recognize or value our gifts and wisdom as elder women. And we begin to believe it—we internalize this oppression, viewing aging with denial and dread, instead of embracing the change and freedom it offers.

Growing old doesn't have to mean an inevitable decline. Positive health habits, including not smoking, exercise, continued mental stimulation, and stress management contribute to vital aging. Our elder years can include a revival of energy and focus, a second adulthood in which new horizons emerge. It is an opportunity to dream our dreams, and fulfill them.

When you are old, what lifestyle do you want? What will it look like? Who will be there? Where? I want you to imagine *your* ideal living situation. The following visualization will tap into your wellspring of inspiration and creativity.

So, please, get comfortable. This visualization will take you about twenty minutes. Put on your favorite soft music, and maybe have a cup of tea nearby. Sit or lie down. Make yourself comfortable with pillows or a blanket if it's cool in the house. If you're by yourself, read each phrase slowly, then daydream. Sometimes this can be awkward, so you may want a friend to read to you slowly, or you can record it yourself. You may want to read each phrase and then write down the thoughts or images that occur to you. That's fine too. You can do this exercise along with a group of women. As with any visualization, there's no right way to do this. Don't think too much—dream!

Please, begin breathing slowly and deeply, letting each breath relax your body and mind. Follow your breath as you inhale and exhale. See each in-breath bringing clear, clean light into your body, each out-breath releasing darkness and tension. Perhaps you need to close your eyes as you let your dreams emerge.

See yourself relaxing more and more with each breath. And even more and more…

Imagine that you are lying in bed with your eyes closed…that relaxed, dreamy state just before you awaken. It's today's date and you are 80 years old.

As you lie there, just before you open your eyes, feel your relaxed body. Feel the muscles in your back, arms and legs. Sense your body and how it is at age 80.

Now imagine that you open your eyes on this morning and look around you.

Notice the light and shadows, colors and shapes of things about you.

Be aware of the temperature, the warmth or coolness on your skin.

Perhaps there are sounds in your environment ...or smells.

You may be alone, or perhaps there's a person or an animal with you.

This is your future, your elder years, and you can have anything you want.

Next imagine that you arise, feeling your body move in the space and time around you. Notice your physical abilities at age 80.

Notice yourself in the mirror. How do you look?

Be aware of the energy flowing inside your body.

And now, imagine the beginning of your day, the rituals and activities, the interactions of early morning.

At the beginning of your day, notice activities of caring for yourself, being cared for, and giving to others—nurturing and nourishment.

Notice the changes in your energy through these activities.

This is your life and you can do anything you want.

Now, continue through the mid-day. Notice your activities.

Notice times of play.

...times of learning.

...times of work.

Notice times of challenge in your day—times of struggle, if they occur, and how you handle them.

Enjoy the times of sharing and joy.

Watch the interactions you have with others. How do these happen? Notice what you and others are doing together and how these connections feel to you.

Be aware of care given and care received.

Feel the energy in your body as it flows and changes throughout the day.

As twilight approaches, you begin your rituals and activities of the evening. Notice what these are.

Be aware of anyone else with you.

Notice your evening meal.

...and time of relaxation.

As it becomes nighttime, you are again in your room preparing for bed. Notice those rituals.

Be aware of the energy in your body at the end of this day, a day created by your wants and needs, the circumstances of your life.

Getting into bed, you are thankful for the relaxation you are experiencing as you begin drifting to sleep with sweet and powerful dreams.

Please take a moment to hold the images you have seen. Prepare to return to the present. Take several deep breaths. Wiggle your fingers and toes, shoulders, hips, and head. Feel yourself solidly on the ground. When you are ready, open your eyes and come back, bringing with you the images and awareness from this visualization.

Now, take a few moments to jot down the impressions, experiences, and feelings that you gained during this exercise. Anything that seemed vivid, positive, or difficult, is noteworthy. The more you record now, the more useful it will be later, because you will be coming back to this visualization repeatedly.

If you are doing this visualization with another person or in a group, you may want to share experiences or you may want to remain quiet, holding your experiences close and savoring them.

REFERENCES

Betty Freidan, *The Fountain of Age.* New York: Simon and Schuster, 1993.

Carolyn G. Heilburn, *The Last Gift of Time: Life Beyond Sixty.* New York: The Dial Press, 1997.

Marge Piercy, *The Longings of Women: A Novel.* New York: Fawcett Columbine, 1994.

Jane Porcino, *Living Longer, Living Better: Adventures in Community Housing for those in the Second Half of Life.* New York: Continuum, 1991.

Gail Sheehy, *New Passages: Mapping Your Life Across Time.* New York: Ballantine Books, 1995.

CHAPTER 1

Could Shared Living Be for You?

The day my friend Kay said to me, "When we're old women, we're going to live together," I considered her suggestion only for a moment before I nodded. I knew that it felt right. I certainly didn't stop to consider how, where, when, or why we would live together, nor did I stop to think about whether shared living suited me, her, or the two of us. These questions arose much later as I began to review my life for information that would help me determine how well I would fare in a collaborative living situation.

In so doing, I kept in mind the importance I placed on my friendships with women. I knew I wanted to deepen those relationships. Having had a long-term marriage meant that I could successfully live with others —I could give and take, maintain my balance, communicate well, and live with self-respect. Obviously, I had some difficulties in my marriage, but on the whole the relationship had worked. Upon consideration, I determined that I was a good candidate for shared living.

Here are some questions that may assist you in determining whether you are suited for collaborative living. If you recorded your thoughts from the visualization in the previous chapter, please put your answers to these questions in the same journal. Throughout this book there will be other questions for you to consider and information that you may want to record. In this way, you will be amassing a personal collection of information about shared living.

Please reflect on the following:

Motivation

- What are your primary reasons for considering collaborative living? Companionship? Economics? Safety and security? Shared values and ideals? If the latter, what are they?
- What reservations do you have about shared living? Loss of privacy? Fears of shared economics? Other reservations?

Past Experiences

Consider your past experiences in living with others, including your family of origin. Also think about previous roommates or partners. Perhaps you'll want to make a time line of your living situations in the past to help you clarify your experiences.

- On the whole, have you been comfortable in shared living situations?
- Were the households you lived in full of crises? Calm and stable? Hierarchical or cooperative?
- Did you experience abuse—psychological, physical, sexual, financial—in any of these situations? Did you cause others harm?
- Have you changed living situations frequently? Or have you lived primarily in long-term households?
- Did anyone abuse alcohol or other drugs in your previous living situations? Have you yourself had substance abuse problems? What's your current use of alcohol or drugs? What are your friends' habits? Do you foresee problems in this area?
- What effect do these past experiences have on you?

From this review, please note the patterns that have emerged over the years. Summarize the habits you have learned that will help you build a harmonious household. These patterns will be your foundation for a collaborative household in the future. Also, notice the habits that you need to overcome in order to create a healthy and comfortable household, such as: do you habitually pay bills late, argue repeatedly with household members, or move every year or two? I encourage you to note the progress you have already made to change those habits that have caused difficulties for you in close relationships. For example, when I learned to let the small stuff go while living with my former husband and stepdaughter, my life and the household became much calmer.

Friendships

- Do you have close, long-term relationships?
- Do you have close women friends now? Do you imagine living with these friends?
- Do you have a full social life now? Or are you a more solitary person? What is a comfortable balance of social and alone time for you? Have you achieved this balance in your current living situation? How would you create this balance in a shared household?
- How do you spend your days? How would this change in a collaborative living situation? Do you hope to socialize outside your home with your housemates; that is, go to

movies, classes, travel, etc., together? Will your housemates be the primary source of companionship?

There are no right answers here. Just notice what you hope for and be prepared to discuss this with others with whom you think you might live. Be clear about your needs for social and alone time. Imagine how you will meet these needs.

Diversity

As you consider these questions, reflect on who you really are, not who or how you think you should be.

- How would you characterize your openness to diversity: racial, ethnic, abilities, age, sexual orientation, class, education, politics?
- Would you be open to living with someone who has significantly different spiritual or religious beliefs and practices from yours?
- How comfortable will you be if the sexual preference of your roommates is different from yours? Race? Age?
- Are there particular abilities or disabilities that you would find difficult to live with? For example, how would you respond to

someone with a visual impairment who asked you to read their mail?

- Do you have abilities or disabilities that others will need to accommodate? Are you comfortable asking for help?
- How much change is reasonably possible for you? How much do you want to change?

Sharing a Household

- What does shared living mean to you?
- Is there a room in the house that you would have difficulty sharing? The kitchen, office, bathroom?
- Do you consider yourself a control freak? Has anyone ever said this of you?
- How easily can you share household responsibilities? Do you tend to overdo? Underdo? How will you balance this?
- Do you hope to share communal meals? How often?
- Do you have particular dietary needs? Preferences? How will you manage these in a shared household? How will you respond to others' dietary needs?

- Are you generally flexible? Too flexible for you own good? Rigid? Do you enjoy spontaneity or structure and planning?
- How will the habits of others affect you? Their music? Friends? Smoking? Drinking? TV usage?
- What experiences have you had sharing money and financial responsibilities? What have you learned from these experiences?
- Do you count every penny? Do hundreds of dollars slip away without your knowing? Does sharing money make you anxious, however carefully this is worked out?
- Do the spending habits of others tend to frighten you? Drive you nuts? Has anyone ever said that your habits drive them nuts?
- Are you handy around the house? Do tools and house repairs bewilder or frighten you? In what ways have you contributed to households—construction, sewing, gardening, cooking, cleaning? Are there household responsibilities you will not do?
- Can you imagine a work exchange, such as care giving, cleaning windows, running

errands, etc., as part of your household? Formally? Informally? How will this influence the financial agreements? Reduce rent? Build equity?

- Do you like pets—cats, dogs, birds, fish? Others? Are you open to sharing your space with animals? How many? What kind? Are you allergic to animals? What kind? How difficult is this for you? Will you care for your housemates' pets when they travel? For how long? How do you respond when pets get ill or die?
- Would you be willing to live in a pet-free household to accommodate others' needs?
- Do you have allergies or sensitivity to products, smells, toxins? How will you address this difficulty in a shared household? The needs of others?

Aging and Care Needs

- Do you have any particular health problems with which you need help? How do you get help if or when you need it?
- If you got the flu next week, or broke a leg or hip, how would you get help? What help

would you want from those with whom you will live?

- How prepared are you to care for someone else? What has been your previous experience with care giving?
- How much time have you spent with people who are old? Have you ever been a caregiver for an old person?
- How willing or prepared are you to care for someone who is dying? Deteriorating mentally?
- What situation do you want for yourself if you deteriorate mentally? When you are dying?
- Under what circumstances of aging would you not want to live collaboratively?

Decision Making

- Which styles of decision making are you familiar with? Authoritarian? Democratic? Talking things out—endlessly? Consensus decision making?
- What method of making decisions would you like to use in a shared living situation?

If you don't already know and use any method of collaborative decision making, how could you learn and practice it now?

Community Building

- What have been your previous experiences with building community? Have you felt a sense of community within women's groups? In social groups? Within parent or advocacy associations? Political groups? Through a religious organization?
- What values or activities do you believe will help to build your household or community?
- Are there spiritual practices that you hope to explore and share in your living situation?

I hope these questions stimulate many thoughts; they do for me each time I review them. From your responses you can identify your strengths as they apply to shared living. And you have also identified areas where you need to do some work. Think about how you can prepare today for shared living in the future. There are seminars or classes you can take which would give you more information and skills. Therapy groups offer an opportunity to practice new communication and other patterns; support groups can also promote change. You can be practicing effective communication, decision making, and problem solving in your work and leisure time activities now. Your perseverance will pay off. Remember, you can come back to these questions again and again to help identify your strengths and needs as you prepare for collaborative living.

From this review you may conclude that you are well-suited to live with others. On the other hand, you may have determined that, however attractive the idea of living with your friends might seem, it would clash with who you are and the way you live. This realization may guide you to live next door to, but not with, your friends.

Once you've set your feet on the path toward collaborative living, you'll want to connect with others who share a similar vision. They will become your circle of support as you consciously plan for your future. I encourage you to discuss your responses to the above questions with potential household members. This exploration may stimulate many wonderful conversations about personal preferences and possibilities on how to live together harmoniously.

REFERENCES

Joe Horne with Leo Baldwin, *Home-Sharing and Other Lifestyle Options*. Washington, DC: American Association of Retired Persons, 1988.

Human Investment Project, Inc. *Homesharing: Successful Strategies*, 1994. This resource guide is available from: Homesharing Help and Information Program, 364 South Railroad Avenue, San Mateo, CA 94401.

CHAPTER 2

Conversations with Other Women

Once it became clear that I wanted to live with my women friends, I began discussing it with them. From these conversations I learned whom I thought I could live with. I could tell, for example, that while several women wanted to live collaboratively, our visions were not similar enough, but we could support one another in our separate dreams.

I encourage you to begin talking about your dreams with women who might be interested. Invite them for tea or give them this book. Together you can reflect on your visions and ideas. Along the way, you may find yourself making new acquaintances with whom you can contemplate living. Please discuss with other women what you learned from the self-assessment questions in the previous chapter; this will be one way to determine how compatible you might be. Some suggestions in this chapter may broaden your conversations.

In time you are likely to find other women who have dreams similar to yours and with whom you believe you could live: this is the time to make a commitment to meet together regularly.

In your group, please consider what sharing means to you. Our culture values sharing, and we teach children to share. Yet a home is prized as a personal possession. Living together, you will be sharing space, time, daily management of the house, financial obligations, decision making, and other ordinary aspects of life. Within a marriage, sharing often means prescribed gender roles: he keeps the financial books, does yard work, and household maintenance; she cooks, cleans the house, and does the laundry. This won't work in a collaborative household for women. (I don't think it works so well in a marriage either, but that's another story.)

So, reflect on what sharing means to you. Does it mean everything being totally equal—money, responsibilities, planning? Does it have a looser definition, that is, a sense of equal sharing, regardless of overt actions or legalities? Is a blend of jointly held property and responsibilities in some areas and a more open sense of sharing in other areas workable for you? In one household, for example, the women rotate the financial record keeping on a monthly basis so that the task will be shared equally. In another, one keeps the books monthly while there is a review by another person semi-annually. How do you want to live collaboratively? What's the balance?

Throughout the process of creating your collaborative living situation you will want to keep notes or minutes of your discussions. Your notes will help you keep track of your ideas and decisions. Later your records will help you formulate guidelines and contracts. Some suggestions for discussion include:

Personal Likes, Dislikes, and Preferences

- smoking and drinking habits
- TV preferences—time watched and volume
- telephone—shared or individual
- music—type and volume
- pets—type, number, and responsibilities
- visitors—frequency and overnight stays
- furniture, appliances (computers), etc. both personal and shared
- cars and parking
- household security—windows, doors, alarms, etc.
- private space and shared space
- private and shared purchase of food, cooking, communal meals

- storage space (private and shared) needed and available
- housekeeping responsibilities
- habits and standards of cleanliness inside and outside the house
- household maintenance and repairs—responsibility and costs
- preferred style of decision making and problem resolution
- needs for privacy—how they will be voiced
- personal difficulties or health problems—how these will be addressed over time
- sharing of household expenses including taxes
- financial record keeping
- desired location of household
- resource contacts—lawyers, bankers, developers, etc.
- planning for future changes in your needs and interests as you age, including increased need for care
- plans upon your death

This is a formidable list; the topics deserve full consideration. So, take your time and enjoy these discussions. In the process, you'll learn new things about yourself and others. For example, one woman with whom I hope to live someday doesn't like onions and I love them. My solution: I cook my food without onions. I've begun growing chives and sprinkle them liberally on my food.

These are typical issues that any couple, members of a family, roommates, or landlord and tenant might discuss. Unfortunately, most people who live together don't discuss these issues up front. I encourage you to discuss them when you are beginning to consider shared living. During these conversations you will establish not only practical matters, such as telephone usage, but also the philosophy of your household. Your discussions can help you to determine if you are compatible in vision and reality. They will help you to determine if you and others can talk openly and honestly and then make adjustments. Conversations about health care needs, styles of decision making, conflict resolution, and plans for changes in health will lead your relationships into more personal areas, building support and collaboration in the process.

You will also want to discuss the notion of shared or common beliefs and values. Are there values that all of you want to live by? For example, one woman is interested in a vegetarian community and growing as much of her food as possible. Another plans to create a household with shared spiritual values and practices—a blend of Jewish traditions and women's spirituality. Another wants to share a household with women who live by feminist values.

Discuss how you will implement your values. You could have daily practices that everyone would join in, such as coffee in the morning. Weekly shared meals might be important. In one household, the members meditate individually every day and have a group mediation over the weekend. Talk about which religious holidays you want to honor and celebrate in your household. Be specific about the activities and practices you want to share. Those collaborative living situations that have incorporated shared values and regular practices to support those values are more cohesive.

As you express your needs and ideas, your circle of support will be growing. Deep transformational forces are at work as you form close bonds. The future of your group is founded on this knowledge.

REFERENCES

Nancy Brandwein, Jill MacNeice and Peter Spiers, *The Group Housing Handbook.* Acropolis Books Ltd., 1982.

Karen Lindsey, *Friends as Family: New Kinds of Families and What They Could Mean for You.* Boston: Beacon Press, 1981.

Teone Tone and Deanna Sclar, *Housemates: A Practical Guide to Living with Other People.* New York: Fawcett Columbine Books, 1985.

CHAPTER 3

Shared Homes

Collaborative living has been with us from early monasteries and nunneries to the commune movement of the sixties and the extensive communities that exist today.

As you become familiar with shared housing models, you can determine which most closely suits you. Some of the basic models for your consideration include shared homes, intentional communities, cooperatives, cohousing communities, community land trusts, and women's land communities.

As I survey the many styles of living communally, I believe that a shared home is the most simple to envision and develop. A shared home is a house that two or more people share. Frequently this home is a single-family dwelling with some modifications. When intentionally developed, a shared home is much more than a house with roommates: the desire to manifest cooperative values and to give the time and effort to maintain those values makes the difference.

The TV hit *The Golden Girls* portrayed one vivid example of a shared home. This situation comedy about a group of older women living together crystallized the dream of many women. One reason I believe that this program was popular is because it tapped into an archetypal longing for companionship that many women have and allowed us to watch this possibility unfold on a weekly basis.

Now, think about the single-family houses you've lived in—two or three bedrooms, one or two bathrooms, kitchen, eating space and a larger living area.

- Would such a house be suitable for a shared living arrangement?
- Would a 10' x 13" bedroom provide adequate private space? Would a traditional house offer enough shared space for your needs? And for others?
- What would be adequate for you? Two adjoining rooms? A private bathroom as well? A small area for private cooking? A separate entrance?
- Will ordinary insulation adequately soften noise from other parts of the house or will more insulation be needed in some areas?

- How many women could a house like this successfully accommodate?
- Is the kitchen large enough to accommodate several people at the same time?
- Would modifications of the house make it suit your needs better?
- Could these modifications be done reasonably?

You may decide that a somewhat larger home modified specifically for shared living or even designed for that purpose will satisfy your needs better than the typical house you've lived in. Ask yourself the questions above. Then examine what modifications would be necessary for a house to be barrier free, accessible for someone with mobility difficulties. While you may be physically okay now, you or someone you live with may not always be. For example, my knees have become stiff and I want a house on one level so that I don't have to be climbing stairs all the time. I want wide doorways and low cabinets. Maybe you couldn't find all of this in an existing house, but you could determine the cost of adapting it. If you're going to build, include these adaptations for accessibility from the start.

There are further considerations. Pets are very important to many women. They meet the need for companionship for older people. A woman I know has five cats and two dogs; she also cares for three horses. The property she lives on can accommodate these animals, but what would be the limits on animals if she were to live in a shared home? Parking could be a problem for shared homes in residential neighborhoods where driveways, garages, or carports generally accommodate only one or two cars. Maybe a third car could park out front, but some areas have restrictions on street parking. However, a house in the country will have adequate parking for many cars.

You'll want to become familiar with zoning ordinances and other restrictions. How many unrelated people can live in a single-family dwelling? A shared house is not a boardinghouse. The laws covering boardinghouses do not apply to a shared home. The existing ordinances in your area may be adequate to include your plans or you may need to work to change them. Some people have ignored the laws, but this is risky.

Is the area around the home you are considering pleasing? Are there sidewalks, parks, or green space? Is the neighborhood friendly? Are the people who live nearby likely to be supportive of a shared home? Outreach or networking with neighbors is important for any nontraditional living situation. Some neighborhoods appear to be open to diversity while others are more rigid. Getting to know your neighbors and helping them to understand and accept your lifestyle is advisable. Your own sense of community may spread as you become acquainted with your neighbors. Perhaps you will have similar interests and concerns that will be the basis for building a strong neighborhood.

Your personal safety in any neighborhood is a crucial factor. Notice whether the area is well maintained. Besides aesthetics, such upkeep discourages crime. You could join a neighborhood watch association. A friend contacted the local police chief about a drug house in her neighborhood. The chief said that ultimately the people in the area needed to take back their community. Initially, a uniformed officer joined the neighbors as they cleaned the area of litter and discarded items. This led to block parties and shared picnics. In time, the area became so visible with people out and about that the drug dealers left. Such community policing programs have been very successful throughout the country.

Is your house near the services you need? Is public transportation available? This is important particularly as we age; low-cost bus or taxi accommodations may be our major means of transportation if we are unable to drive ourselves. One of my friends lives in a suburb, but someday hopes to move into town where she can walk to nearby stores and cafes.

The cost of a shared home can vary. You will find that there are some ways to help fund collaborative living projects described in Chapter 10.

If the property has a single owner, legally the household is a landlord-tenant situation despite any personal agreements that you may make. You may want to own the property while your friends rent, or you might prefer to be a renter in such a household. Do you want the house to function in an egalitarian way regardless of legalities? Is it truly possible to create equality without contracts? The most common legal method for shared ownership of property is tenants-in-common. Cooperative, partnership, or non-profit corporations may be appropriate in some situations as well. These alternatives will also be discussed in Chapter 10.

Thorough planning before you begin living together will help you avoid unpleasantness caused by inadequate or poorly designed space, poor location, or inappropriate legal arrangements. Knowing what would suit you best will help you to make design choices.

From the women who have contacted me, I know that many shared households exist. If you hope to join an existing household, as opposed to creating one, ask around. Organizations such as the National Shared Housing Resource Center and their regional offices can help you to find shared situations. The household you find may or may not fit your needs, but it may be worth investigating.

Barb, a warm-hearted woman in her early sixties, called after hearing me do a radio interview about shared living. She lived with a friend for fifteen years. Her experiences were typical of many women who have shared their homes with friends.

These two women became friends over several years because of common interests—spirituality and natural healing. When Barb's children left home, she and her friend wanted the economic ease and companionship that collaborative living offered, so they began living in Barb's home. Her friend paid rent. While an inequality in power existed, they made many decisions jointly. Later they moved to Santa Fe, buying a home together using Barb's equity as a down payment. The other woman was new to home ownership and somewhat shocked by the economic responsibilities of upkeep and repair. Barb continued to pay for some of the larger expenses, such as a new roof, because she had the resources to do so and was at ease sharing them. Although initially her friend felt uncomfortable because she was not assuming an equal share of the financial responsibilities, in time these feelings resolved themselves.

The companionship has been wonderful, they say, but there have been some disadvantages. Because they are so close, sometimes they have not reached out to create new friendships and living with a woman friend can often keep men away. Sometimes people assume that Barb is a lesbian.

They have not considered how they will accommodate their needs as they age. They are both very healthy, but they live outside Santa Fe, making access to services—transportation, health care, social, etc.—more difficult. "We'll see," they say.

Another woman has owned several shared homes over the past twenty years. Initially she wanted to buy a large house in Oakland. The only way she could do so was to rent space to other women. As the owner, she established a landlord and tenant relationship with those women. She described some wonderful long-term relationships with several tenants over the years. She has also had frequent turnover, some people were just passing through. While these residents share the physical space of this house, they really aren't close. This requires more collaboration. Nevertheless, this situation suits this woman's personality and interests as well as those of her tenants.

My friend, Jo, has lived in several types of shared situations. She owned a home when her son was young. Then women joined them renting their rooms. Now she prefers the freedom of being a renter herself.

She is able to move whenever the mood strikes her—she's lived in wonderful locations such as the coasts of Oregon and Maui. When the roof leaks, she doesn't have to pay for it or have to get it fixed. In contrast to the landlord and tenant situation described above, however, this woman looks for households that have a family feel. She wants frequently shared meals and communal responsibility. Shared time just hanging out together as well as formal meetings to discuss various needs and develop strategies for addressing these are fundamental to her. The households that Jo has chosen and helped to create have been functionally egalitarian whatever the ownership. Despite her frequent moves, she has been able to find women with similar interests in each location and is clearly adept at creating strong shared homes.

As you consider developing a shared home, please remember that there is no right or wrong way. Your task is to structure your living situation in a way that best suits you and your housemates. In such an environment you can flourish.

Key Characteristics of Shared Homes

- *Structure*—Generally one house, often an existing home.

- *Number of people*—Generally 2–3.
- *Location*—Usually urban.
- *Cost*—Varies.
- *Availability*—May be hard, but you can always create your own.
- *Support Services*—City services such as transportation, health care, etc.; discuss public supplied support through the aging and dying process.
- *Guidelines*—Generally unavailable; attempt to develop these.
- *Legal Arrangements*—Tenants-in-common, landlord/tenant, partnership, non-profit.
- *Special Features*—Perhaps the most accessible model to many women because it can be developed anywhere.
- *Special Concerns*—Neighborhood relationships and safety, zoning ordinances.

In contrast to a shared home, the next chapter will consider community lifestyles. Communities contain more people than a shared home.

REFERENCES

Deborah Chalfie, *The Real Golden Girls: The Prevalence and Policy Treatment of Midlife and Older People Living in Nontraditional Households.* A Publication of the Women's Initiative, Office of Special Activities. Washington, DC: American Association of Retired Persons, 1995.

National Shared Housing Resource Center, 431 Pine Street, Burlington, VT 05401, Phone: 1-800-862-2727

Eric Raimy, *Shared Houses, Shared Lives: The New Extended Families and How They Work.* New York: J.P. Tarcher, Inc., 1979.

CHAPTER 4

Intentional Communities

Community doesn't occur because people live in the same building or next door, as any apartment dweller or suburbanite will tell you. Real community requires effort: working together toward a common goal; sharing values and activities; communicating in healthy ways; making fair and inclusive decisions; and successfully resolving conflicts. Shared activities are also necessary for community to develop, such as designing and tending a garden, monthly hikes, and social occasions. Unity comes as the sense of connection and companionship grow.

The term "intentional community" describes a purposefully created community. Some groups refer to themselves as intentional communities, while others call themselves cooperatives, cohousing communities, community land trusts, ecovillages, or women's land communities. Each intentional community has its individual purpose and style.

Most of us have built community, somehow and somewhere. Quilting bees, shared cooking, canning, or caring for the ill were sources of community in the past for many women, as well as churches, bridge clubs, and reading groups. Car pools, bake sales, and the PTA have helped to create community. More recently, women have developed crisis centers for victims of abuse or rape. For those women and the people they served, community building occurred in the process of the work they were doing together. Neighborhood watch associations have helped to build a sense of community among residents. In all these instances, people worked together toward a common goal. Please remember your experiences in the past creating and being in community; you can draw from the successes and difficulties of those efforts. You might list these experiences in your journal.

Often one individual, someone with a dream that inspires others, starts a community. Generally this person has passion for the goal at hand, charisma, considerable leadership ability, and energy. You may be that vision carrier for your group, or perhaps someone else may be the leader. Others may become empowered to complement the initial leader. Don't underestimate the amount of work involved in building community.

Intentional communities vary greatly. Some are relatively small, eight to ten members, while others are very large with over a hundred members. They generally include individual homes and community buildings. Shared facilities may include a large communal kitchen, library, shop, storage space, gardens, etc. The cost can vary according to the lifestyle of the community and availability of housing. In some groups, economic resources are pooled while others share money only for the purpose of mortgage payments. Legally some communities are structured as cooperatives, while others are non-profit corporations.

Some communities are relatively separate from the people and society around them while others are connected. In some groups members strictly adhere to doctrines and lifestyle, while in others there is more flexibility and individuality. Whatever the differences in values, organization, or lifestyle, all communities share one common value: cooperation.

Another feature common to all communities is the need to develop clear community guidelines about problems. These issues include:

- clarification of intention and lifestyle
- development of a standard of living
- consensus regarding decision-making models
- definition and development of financial stability

- agreement about common activities and responsibilities
- conditions and procedures to join or leave the community
- provision of resources to community members
- agreement about raising children or including or excluding them in the community
- development of policies which address the needs of community members as they age

The purpose, decisions, and guidelines that a group establishes not only give focus and direction to the community, but also help potential members to determine whether they will fit in that community. The vision and guidelines also direct the choice of property, organizational, and legal arrangements.

However, often in a rush of idealism, the hard work of clarifying a group's intent and the development of written guidelines and contracts is incomplete. The communities that are the most stable have developed clear guidelines that members agree to follow. Vagueness may indicate covert intentions or instability, conscious or unconscious.

Most well-established communities will tell you their guidelines to assist you in developing your own community. You can locate many existing groups through the *Communities Directory*, compiled and published by the Fellowship for Intentional Communities, listed in the references at the end of this chapter. The most recent edition of the directory listed over 350 communities with varying intentions, size, locations, and organizational structures. Reading their journal, *Communities: Journal of Cooperative Living*, I've come to understand what the breadth of community means in allowing for individual creativity and individual needs.

I urge you to investigate both the idea of community as well as the reality of the communities that already exist. Many intentional communities welcome visitors; again, you can find these through the *Communities Directory*. Taking advantage of these opportunities will help you gather invaluable information about community lifestyles. You will be able to experience community in action, talk with others about your vision, discuss guidelines that they have found useful, and ask questions. You will also be developing good allies in the world of community living.

By reading about and visiting established communities, you may find that a group with values and interests similar to yours already exists and that joining it may suit your needs. You may find that you are compatible with their stated intentions. You can learn how you may become a member, and what your responsibilities and costs will be. Most groups have established a period of time with increasing levels of commitment.

Over time, both the community and prospective members can determine if they will be compatible. If unresolvable problems develop, the community may decide that a possible member will not fit, and follow its procedures to disengage from future association. An individual may, on the other hand, make that decision.

Unfortunately, we've all heard examples of community disasters—unresolvable conflicts, disenchantment, and failures. People in community often live differently from society. Communities develop their own norms; from the outside these ways can appear strange. Often, religious communities have been the focus of criticism: Amish or Shaker groups have experienced prejudice. Unfortunately, outsiders may accuse a group of being a cult because they do not understand or agree with a community's values or behavior. Intolerance can lead to false accusations.

There are, however, untrustworthy "gurus," dangerous cults, and situations that are better avoided. Realistically, how could you recognize and avoid dangerous individuals or hurtful situations?

- Stay aware!
- Question authority, particularly if that authority professes a unique relationship with God or claims that you can connect to spirit only through that individual.
- Avoid violence, people with guns, or suicide pacts.
- Watch, and thoughtfully consider, what happens without letting your emotions overwhelm your common sense.
- Don't give your money away unless you're "giving" it away; know what your money is buying.
- Don't get close to people with whom you are uncomfortable or those whom you don't trust; be willing to leave situations that are continually in conflict.
- Recognize your vulnerabilities: abuse or neglect in your early life, or more recent educational, vocational, or relationship difficulties may leave you discouraged and at risk.
- Trust your intuition.

You may want to consider creating your own community and then affiliating with others to make a larger association. The Federation of Egalitarian Communities is one such network of five groups. Their publication *Sharing the Dream* states,

> *"Because we share so much, and because we are committed to a vision of community which transcends our individual groups, we have joined together to cooperate on publications, conferences, recruitment efforts, community support systems including health care, and a variety of other mutually supportive activities. Our aim is not only to help each other, we want to help more people discover the advantages of a communal alternative, and to promote the evolution of a more egalitarian world."*

Twin Oaks in Virginia was the first community in this network. Organized in 1967, it currently has 90 members. Acorn, an associated feminist community that began in 1993, has approximately 20 members. Such successful communities are valuable resources.

Most communities have not had to deal with the needs of the elderly within their membership. This will change, however, as the baby boom generation ages.

MAKING THEIR DREAM A REALITY

I watched two of my friends keep their dream and build a community. For nearly two years they met with other men and women to discuss their interest in living in community. Once they had a sense of purpose, they began to search for rural property and finally found suitable land. Ultimately, only three women bought into the community. Before and after this purchase, the women met monthly to work out their rules. They scheduled monthly community meetings and work parties around weekends when they were all on the property.

One woman moved into an existing structure, the community house, shortly after they bought the property. From there she supervised and helped to construct her home at the base of a nearby hill. During this time, other community members also used the community house on weekends and other times. Together they renovated a detached room off the community house to accommodate a library and a guest room. Now that the woman has moved into her house, the community house is available for others. Three years after their purchase, they still meet one day a month; while the focus of these meetings has changed over the years, the need for them continues. Clearly, living in community means devoting time and loving energy to nurturing relationships with others as well as to the land and buildings of the community.

For about six months I met with a group of women who were living or had lived in some sort of shared living situation or intentional community. These gatherings were rich: I learned a tremendous amount from these women. In turn, they reported feeling supported and gaining useful insights from other women.

Most of the women agreed that when problems occurred in the early stages of creating community, they tended to avoid them instead of addressing them openly. As women, we have been encouraged to "make nice," whereas honest discussion of concerns as they arise is necessary.

Lee and Kathleen left a feminist community that then collapsed. The initiator of the community began to believe herself a leader rather than an equal partner. There were no written guidelines or agreements; they had merely trusted one another to create a community of equality. In a short time, this undefined arrangement became intolerable. It was an expensive endeavor, emotionally and financially. After a time of withdrawal from community living, however, both women were again open to living with others, though they wanted a different model with written guidelines. Kathleen now lives in a rural area; community is "unintentionally" developing among the women in her area as they support one another through the hardships of isolated living. Her neighbors are open to helping one another and joining in fun times as well.

Barbara experienced increasing conflicts in her community which led to mediation and then to litigation, because the women had different individual values about the land and its use. There was also verbal abuse and destruction of property. She noted that in the early stages of the development of this community she wanted to avoid legalities, but afterwards she found them useful. She remains optimistic about again being part of a community. Having lived alone most of her life, she feels that this conflict provided an opportunity to learn how to speak up for herself rather than to accept other people's wishes. She has gained confidence in expressing her needs in all aspects of her life and she has come to rethink the conflict as a personal crossroads—a time to grow.

Another woman described a linear, male model of decision making in her community of both women and men, with a general undervaluing of women's experiences and gifts. She hopes she might encourage a more inclusive way of making decisions.

Moon lived in lesbian communities for over twenty years. She'd seen women and problems come and go. In her late fifties, she was the oldest woman in her group and had also lived in that community longer than any other resident. The younger women were often insistent on trying out their ideas before considering the group's past. She found it valuable to meet other older women who valued her wisdom.

All of these women agreed that they could not look to their shared household or community for their entire support. Outside friendships, family, and activities were important. Several found that individual therapy helped them through times of community conflict. They further agreed that shared activities, such as communal meals or yard work, rituals, and spiritual celebrations were vital for the bonds to develop. They acknowledged the importance of written guidelines to establish and solidify their relationships.

Despite their prior difficulties, every woman in this group still wanted to live collaboratively. In retrospect, they found that the personal rewards—companionship, growth, a sense of connection—far outweighed the problems they had encountered.

Key Characteristics of Intentional Communities

- *Structures*—Individual homes and several shared community buildings such as meeting rooms, large kitchen, library, etc.
- *Size*—Small to large groups, from 5 or 6 to 100+.
- *Location*—Generally rural.
- *Cost*—Varies.
- *Availability*—Many communities exist and are being developed.
- *Support Services*—Large communities often offer some services. Find out specifically what is available and how each community meets the needs of aging and dying members.
- *Guidelines*—Generally available.
- *Legal Arrangement*—Cooperative, non-profit.
- *Special Features*—Communities generally have specific intent and focus, such as addressing environmental concerns, shared spiritual values, etc.
- *Special Concerns*—Time needed to build a

community; potential for misunderstanding from external or internal conflicts.

Creating or joining a community comes from the desire for sharing and harmony. It takes perseverance to be a community member.

The women in the above group had lived in very different types of communities—an intentional community, cohousing, and women's communities. In the next two chapters, these models of community living will be explored.

REFERENCES

Communities: Journal of Cooperative Living. This wonderful journal is available from: The Fellowship for Intentional Community, Route 1, Box 155, Rutledge, MO 63563. Web site: http://www.well.com/user/cmty/fic/

Communities Directory, also available from the Fellowship for Intentional Community address above. It lists over 350 communities cross-referencing information like urban/rural, percentage of women and the focus of community. It has been an invaluable resource to me.

Federation of Egalitarian Communities, 138 Twin Oaks Rd., Louisa, VA 23093. Phone: 540-894-5126. Web Page: http://www.crl.com/eastwind/fec.htm E-mail: FEC@ic.org

Kay Leigh Hagan, "Heart Sisters: Loving Each Other Over Time" in *Fugitive Information: Essays from a Feminist Hothead*, San Francisco: Harper Collins, 1993.

Corine McLaughlin and Gordon Davidson, *Builders of the Dawn: Community Lifestyles in a Changing World.* Summertown, TN: Book Publishing Company, 1985. This inspiring book captured the spirit of community better than any other book that I read.

CHAPTER 5

Cooperatives, Cohousing, and More

When I began investigating community lifestyles, I had no idea of the variety of possibilities that already existed. Cooperatives, cohousing communities, community land trusts, ecovillages, and others are all different kinds of intentional communities. They are different in their intent, social organization, physical structure, and contractual nature. This chapter will compare these models.

COOPERATIVE HOUSING

"Cooperative," or "co-op," may apply to any business—a farm, child care facility, food market—as well as a type of housing arrangement. A co-op is designed to meet common economic, social, and cultural needs through a jointly-owned, democratically-controlled enterprise.

In a co-op, housing is not regarded as a financial investment, but as a way of securing decent, affordable shelter. Most homeowners expect to make a profit when they sell a home; co-ops generally eliminate the profit motive and, thus, controlling housing costs.

Individuals create a housing co-op by forming a cooperative corporation designed to own and operate housing. Members of the cooperative, who are the shareholders of the corporation, elect a board of directors to guide the organization. Members own, maintain, and run their own household or housing project through a democratic process of decision making. Socializing, sharing daily responsibilities, and long-term planning nurture the connection among the members. A cooperative may function communally or as independent housing units. The co-op assesses a monthly fee from its members to pay for necessities such as maintenance and repairs, landscaping, etc. Residents divide the mortgage payment among themselves. The board may hire an administrator to do the bookkeeping, tenant selection, and other functions, or the residents may assume responsibility for these activities themselves. Members can keep their costs low by contributing labor instead of hiring others to do needed work. Activities that are often unpaid or underpaid outside a cooperative, such as shopping, laundry, and cooking, are valued in most co-ops; they are counted as contributions along with all other tasks.

Legally, housing co-ops are either "cooperative housing corporations" or "limited-equity housing cooperatives." A cooperative housing corporation generally applies to housing over 25 units; whereas, a limited-equity housing cooperative is for smaller groups. When members live in the housing, and most do, they are owner-occupants or member-residents.

The principles common to all cooperatives include:

- open membership (non-discriminatory)
- democratic control
- agreed upon returns on financial investments
- education of the membership in cooperative principles
- cooperation among members
- association with other cooperatives

High-rise apartments or exclusive housing projects sometimes incorporate as cooperatives to keep the cost of housing down. However, most often these do not operate communally. There are also some small communal households organized as co-ops, offering both economic and social benefits to the members. Moderate-income housing has interested some groups. There are some other groups that address the special needs of the elderly, physically, mentally, or emotionally challenged people.

A co-op may be in one location or have several households scattered in various locations. Scattered site cooperatives have a common corporation to manage the several houses. Groups in Los Angeles, Madison, and other areas have developed this type of cooperative.

The Madison Community Co-op (MCC) includes ten households. While students and parents with young children comprise most of these homes, each has its own character. A common interest in social justice attracted the members of the Emma Goldman Co-op. Ofek Shalom is a Jewish household. The Women's Co-op is for women who want to create a safe and supportive home. The umbrella group, MCC, offers support, long-term stability, growth, and membership in a national co-op community. MCC has begun to diversify their membership to include more groups, including possibly a crone's nest—a household for old women. MCC offers start-up loans and legal assistance to new co-ops in Madison.

Large housing cooperatives specifically designed for senior citizens have begun to flourish. Homestead Cooperatives, located primarily in Minnesota and Iowa, is a unique senior cooperative. It accommodates members in rural areas with fully accessible apartments and needed support services so that they can continue living independently. Thus, people who no longer want to live in single-family housing are able to stay in their home town. Homestead Cooperatives, along with financial support from regional companies and organizations, provides technical assistance and seed capital to groups that want to develop cooperatives in their area.

Nationwide funding for cooperatives is available through organizations such as the National Cooperative Bank. Affordable Housing Programs of the Federal Home Loan Bank has provisions for cooperatives. Co-ops can use resources from Community Development Funds and Neighborhood Housing Associations. Private lending institutions are showing increased interest in financing co-ops. The National Association of Housing Cooperatives offers technical assistance to groups interested in establishing cooperatives and securing funding.

Key Characteristics of Cooperatives

- *Structures*—Can be one household or multiple housing units such as apartments; each co-op shares some rooms or buildings; can be scattered site.
- *Size*—Varies, can be 3 to 5 people or 100+.
- *Location*—Are urban and rural.
- *Cost*—Varies but one intent of co-ops is to control housing costs.

- *Availability*—Co-ops are increasingly popular and more common in northeastern U.S.
- *Support Services*—Individual households may offer a few services on an individual basis; larger communal co-ops often offer more services. Ask specifically about the services for elderly and dying members.
- *Guidelines*—Are generally available.
- *Legal*—Cooperative structure.
- *Special Features and Concerns*—A cooperative can be many things in different situations, so ask about the purpose and how each operates.

COHOUSING

Many women dream of living alone, but don't want isolation. Cohousing is one solution as it encourages interhousehold support.

Cohousing is the American name of a particular type of intentional community whose roots began in the early seventies in Denmark where it was called *Beofaellesskab*, meaning "living community." Cohousing communities have self-sufficient, privately owned homes built around shared land and facilities—including a communal kitchen and dining hall, children's play rooms, workshops, guest rooms, laundry, gardens, picnic and play areas. Common parking areas are exterior to the dwellings, and pathways to the homes encourage interaction with neighbors. Meals are shared several times a week. These are central to the community.

The physical design and layout of the structures encourage interhousehold connection and are the distinguishing features of cohousing. The shared development and management of the community further enhance the sense of association. In contrast to cooperatives, cohousing has no intention to affect the cost of housing. Cohousing communities generally cost in the moderate to upper range, in part because they are recently constructed. Although some attempt to develop affordable cohousing is emerging. In addition to the individual cost of building or purchasing a house, a community fee is assessed. The legal structure for a cohousing community is generally a condominium.

Most cohousing communities begin with twenty to thirty interested individuals joining to design the community and then guiding all aspects of its development. This is a tremendous task, taking several years from the initial dream to completion. Today there are about forty different cohousing communities in the United States.

The basic characteristics of cohousing include:

- *Participatory Process*—Community members design and plan the development of the property.
- *Intentional Neighborhood Design*—Architecture and physical design encourage community involvement.
- *Extensive Common Facilities*—Common areas designed for daily use supplement private living space.
- *Complete Resident Management*—All decisions of common concern are made at community meetings.

In Santa Fe, New Mexico, there are two cohousing communities. Two of my friends who lived in one of these dreamed of having their own space while participating in community. One loves community: "It's safe because you know your neighbors and they all watch out for each other. Also the diversity of personalities and ages requires learning to accept others and communicate with them—to develop healthy ways of being together." It's not all easy, however. The other woman describes a male dominance over feminine values in the community. For example, the community accepts construction activities for work credits, but not cooking for a community member who is ill. Should we be surprised that the inequalities in our larger society appear in a smaller community as well? She hopes that because of the smaller size of this cohousing community and its commitment to cooperation, new ways of collaboration can develop.

I talked with a woman from Santa Rosa, California, who was part of a group that tried for over a year to develop a women's cohousing community. The group concluded that a "women only" development would be discriminatory, and most of the women were reluctant to invest their resources in this way. Perhaps a small, private community organized along the lines of the cohousing model would be both legal and successful, though I am aware of no such group. This disappoints me as I really like the cohousing model of organization.

Key Characteristics of Cohousing

- *Structures*—Individual houses surround shared facilities such as a large kitchen, community rooms, laundry facilities, etc.
- *Size*—Is about 25 to 40 households.
- *Location*—Generally urban.

- *Cost*—Is moderate to high end though some affordable housing and rental units are included.
- *Availability*—About 40 communities exist around the country.
- *Support Services*—Few are organized. Ask about specific accommodations for elderly and dying residents; otherwise, members must use city services.
- *Guidelines*—Generally available.
- *Legal*—Condominium or cooperative structure.
- *Special Features*—Specific design and management characteristics.
- *Special Concerns*—May reflect gender equality; community support services needed; few communities available to lower income and aging individuals.

COMMUNITY LAND TRUSTS

A Community Land Trust (CLT) is a non-profit corporation designed to buy and hold land for the benefit of the community, thus providing secure, affordable access to land and housing. This model of shared ownership honors the environment through careful decision making regarding land use. Traditional private ownership of land encourages speculation (buy low-sell high), absentee ownership, and misuse of the environment. Like cooperatives, Community Land Trusts remove the potential profit motive. Land development projects are designed to benefit the community.

Community Land Trusts may incorporate various types of housing—individual homes, cohousing, or cooperatives. Individual buyers own their homes but lease the land, usually for 99 years, from the CLT. Homeowners pay significantly less for their housing because a cooperative or non-profit cooperation purchased the land; residents still receive the equity and tax benefits of ownership, however. Upon sale, owners get back their investment and perhaps some compensation for inflation, but not the type of increase that many homeowners expect when they sell their property. Restricting the resale price assures continued affordable housing. A CLT can vary in size. Because of their interest in preserving the environment, the use of their acreage is carefully controlled.

Sources of initial funding for a CLT include banks and traditional housing lenders as well as foundations, religious organizations, individual contributions, and government agencies. Once operating, a CLT may generate funding through lease fees, rental income, and membership dues. The Institute for Community Economics is a valuable resource for information regarding the development and funding of a Community Land Trust.

CLTs attempt to meet the needs of people financially unable to purchase homes. Women, because of their economic status in society, are finding CLTs an important means to home ownership. As you will see in the next chapter, many of the women's land communities have organized as Community Land Trusts.

Key Characteristics of Community Land Trusts

- *Structures*—Are multiple, individual, and shared.
- *Size*—Can be small, 5 to 8 individuals, or larger.
- *Location*—Is generally rural.
- *Cost*—Varies. The intent is to provide affordable housing for future generations.
- *Availability*—CLTs are not as common yet, but are growing in popularity.
- *Support Services*—Ask each community about your specific interests.

- *Guidelines*—Are generally written.
- *Legal*—Non-profit or cooperative.
- *Special Features*—In addition to affordable housing, CLTs are focused on preserving the environment; many women's communities are set up as a CLT.

ECOVILLAGES

The members of an ecovillage share strong values and practices centered on sustaining life and the environment. An ecovillage, eco-city, or eco-community is a compact arrangement of houses, green space, agriculture, and small businesses. Solar or other energy-efficient methods of power, nonpolluting water systems, and controlled activities help to preserve the environment. Residents consider social, economic, and physical impacts of all community design elements toward the goal of sustainability. In an ecovillage, residents live close together and grow much of their food. The physical and economic systems are designed to strengthen both the family and community. Groups are generally moderate in size. Cooperative and non-profit corporations are the common legal structure. As this model of community is very new, the costs are unclear, but efforts toward affordable housing are common.

Every ecovillage is unique. Some, like EcoVillage at Ithaca in New York, start from the ground up. Under development now, this community is an educational model for other ecovillages. Consisting of one hundred fifty households, a cohousing arrangement will occupy 20 percent of the 176 acres. The remaining land will be agricultural and open space.

Other communities, such as the Los Angeles Ecovillage at Bimini-White House Place, are a "retrofit"; that is, various new ecological systems that were not available when areas were originally built are now being added. Plans include the reclamation of gray water and the use of renewable energy systems. The current apartments will become affordable cooperatives. This eco-village will have a community center, childcare, youth and other community services. Decision making by consensus will help create the social community. Education and training in various aspects of social and environmental sustainablity will be ongoing.

The ecovillage concept is international, with communities developing in countries such as Denmark, Germany, Australia, Israel, and Canada. The Third International EcoCities Conference, held in Yoff, Senegal, in 1996, included representatives from 27 countries. This is a new movement; most villages are in the planning and acquisition stage. Interest in this model is increasing as more people recognize the present environmental crisis.

Key Characteristics of Ecovillages

- *Structures*—Include several individual homes, community buildings, and businesses.
- *Size*—Is moderate size, 25 to 75 households.
- *Location*—Is both urban and rural.
- *Cost*—Is moderate.
- *Availability*—Ecovillages are a newly developing lifestyle option; few exist as yet.
- *Support Services*—The intent is to have services available. Ask specifically about services for the elderly and dying.
- *Guidelines*—Are generally available.
- *Legal*—Cooperative and non-profit.
- *Special Features*—The focus is on sustaining the environment with a variety of environmental and land use measures.
- *Special Concerns*—As a new model, long-term viability is as yet unclear.

AND MORE

Still other types of community models exist and, presumably, new ideas are evolving all the time. Elder Cottage Housing Opportunity, (ECHO), originated in Australia as "granny flats." In Hawai'i, "ohana," or family units, are common. ECHO units are small self-contained apartments built behind a family home. These accessory apartments are often prefabricated, installed on the property, and removed when they are no longer needed. A complete ECHO unit is fully accessible and barrier-free. A cluster of several ECHO units can form a small community.

A Mutual Housing Association (MHA) is a non-profit, membership-controlled corporation designed to own and manage affordable housing. An MHA can provide ongoing services and continuing assistance to affiliated co-ops in times of need.

In these various housing models, one type will often incorporate another, similar to the inclusion of cooperatives within a Community Land Trust. The major differences between various models lie in their purpose, type of property ownership, guidelines regarding resale, and emphasis on sustainable living. The physical and social organization of each model is different as well. All these innovations grew out of dissatisfaction with isolated urban and suburban living and a concern for the environment.

Becoming familiar with the values, design, social and legal aspects of each model will help you decide if one of these models will suit your needs. Ken Norwood at the Shared Living Resource Center is an invaluable resource on these models for collaborative living. The *Cooperative Housing Compendium* is an excellent book that describes each of these models in more detail.

All of these models embrace social aspects of community building. From the strong relationships formed between members, the technical aspects of the community can evolve. An easily understood philosophy, good communication skills, and cooperative activities are fundamental to all community building—whatever the model. Without these values and skills, it doesn't matter what kind of water system you develop; genuine community lies in relationships of the people.

The variety of community models as described here demonstrates the growth of interest in community living. You will need to be clear about your intention so as to match it with the type of community you develop or join. With clear intent and right action, your community will blossom.

REFERENCES

Lottie Cohen and Lois Arkin, eds. *Cooperative Housing Compendium: Resources for Collaborative Living*. Center for Cooperatives, UC Davis, Davis, CA 95616. This was an invaluable resource—with good descriptions of types of communities, ownership models, and suggestions for financing collaborative living.

Shared Living Resource Center, 237 Shattuck Ave., Berkeley, CA 94704. Phone: 510-548-6608.

Cohousing:

Kathryn McCamant and Charles Durrett with Ellen Hertzman, *CoHousing: A Contemporary Approach to Housing Ourselves,* 2nd ed. Berkeley: Ten Speed Press, 1994.

Cohousing Network (Journal and other resources), P.O. Box 2584, Berkeley, CA 94702.
Web site: http://www.cohousing/org

Community Land Trusts:

The Institute for Community Economics (ICE), 57 School Street, Springfield, MA 01105.

Cooperatives:

National Association of Housing Cooperative, 1614 King Street, Alexandria, VA 22314.

The Co-op Resource Center, 1442 A Walnut Street, #415, Berkeley, CA 94709.

Cooperative Resources and Services Project (CRSP), P.O. Box 27731, Los Angeles, CA 27731.

Ecovillages:

Ecovillage Network of the Americas, P.O. Box 90, The Farm, Summertown, TN 38483-0090. E-mail: ecovillage@thefarm.org

McGee Foundation, P.O. Box 56756, Washington, DC 20040. E-mail: oegeberg@capacess.org. This organization has a startup letter for ecovillages and a sheet of tips for neighborhood organizing.

CHAPTER 6

Women's Land Communities

The terms "women's land" and "lesbian land" are generally used synonymously. Most of these communities were begun by lesbians; yet, several women's land communities are open to all women. Some women's land communities were intentionally developed by and for both lesbian and straight women.

Women's land communities were a natural outgrowth of the early lesbian and feminist rights movement in this country and Europe when many lesbians began to search for a space safe from sexist and heterosexist oppression. Like many other dreams of community, the beginning of women's land groups was idealistic. These women dreamed about living in harmony and treating one another with respect and equality. Their hope was to rise above the abuse of power endemic in the larger society and to live more supportively. Their dream didn't always work: some patriarchal ways were expressed in their communities. However, despite these challenges, many of the early women's communities continue, and new groups are forming today as well.

While writing this book I visited ARF, a women's rural Community Land Trust in the mountains outside Santa Fe, and talked with friends there.

Each women's land community has its own story, character, and intent. Some groups may have begun on acreage owned by one woman, while in others women have jointly leased or purchased property. Some groups emerged spontaneously while others took years to form. Virtually all women's land communities are in rural areas. They vary in acreage and members.

Typically, there are five or six women in a community. Most of the communities are managed by the residents, though some have a non-profit board of directors. Many are set up as a Community Land Trust. Costs are generally low as it is understood in these communities that the economic inequities that exist in the larger society often leave women with few personal resources. Each group has certain characteristics and interests. One community has goats, while several maintain organic gardens, hiking trails, and swimming holes. Some groups emphasize the inclusion of women with disabilities. Many groups have a goddess-centered focus.

As with any community in a rural area, a primary concern of most women's land groups has been their economic sustainability. Many groups, such as Camp

Sister Spirit, Owl, and D.O.E. Farm, rent seasonal camping and retreat space. Some groups maintain bed and breakfast accommodations. We'moon Healing Ground produces *We'moon: Gaia Rhythms for Womyn*, an annual astrological appointment book. One group that does not have year-round residents reported, "There is potential for farming or any number of cottage industries, but these would take an investment of time, energy, and money to get going. So far, we've not been able to support ourselves on the land throughout the year." Thus many successful groups are within a reasonable driving distance of a city or town with employment opportunities.

With varying degrees of success, women's land community members address their concerns about all the "isms"—class, economic, gender, racial, ability, and age. Some efforts have been successful, others have had great difficulty, and some have failed.

Lesbian communities have had specific concerns that other women may not share. Some women want to be separatist, while others who have sons or other close male family members or friends want to raise their sons on the land and be able to have men visit. In some groups boys up to a particular age may be allowed; in others, men may be allowed on the land with advance notice. In still others, no men will be allowed under any circumstance. I know of one group, separatist for many years, that was opened to men at the request of a member who was dying; the ongoing respect and love within the community allowed the group to suspend their agreed-upon policy for a brief time. These groups represent the best efforts of women to create harmony in a new way.

As many women living on the land are reaching middle and old age, more residents are talking about the needs of the elderly. The women at the Susan B. Anthony Memorial Unrest Home, begun in 1979, are themselves aging. Their members are feminists, both lesbian and straight. They hope to respond to the emerging desire for women's community as we age. At Spinsterhaven, Inc. the mission is to "create and maintain nurturing community homes for aging women and women with disabilities." This group, for women 55 and older, acknowledges that the community needs of old women are generally unmet and encourages women to "put together exactly what you want." I suspect that the focus on aging will increase as the baby boom generation ages.

ONE WOMAN'S EXPERIENCE

My friend Moon first lived in community with her husband and two daughters outside San Francisco. After coming out as a lesbian, she, along with twelve other women and their seven children, built the community of Aurora. From there she went to Momma Mountain. When it dissolved and the women dispersed, she spent ten years traveling in her van from one community to another, finally settling in the mountains outside of Santa Fe at ARF.

Moon described the early efforts of women's communities and the innovations they initiated; many that we now consider the norm. They conducted two kinds of meetings; some that focused on business, others that focused on feelings. They shared child rearing, used co-counseling and agreements to mediate conflicts. She described clean and sober areas designed for women who were coming out of addiction and the conflicts over partying. Some communities shared everything: food, responsibilities, and money; in one, the "house mother of the month" collected money and paid the bills. In another group a school was founded for their children as well as children living nearby.

From her earliest experiences Moon counted 50 women in her "tribe," whether they lived on the land or not. "I always wanted to go home—to my people—and that's what lesbian land has given me," she reflected.

THE LARGER LESBIAN COMMUNITY

Because lesbians are a minority group that experiences prejudice and oppression everywhere, within the group there is a sense of community. Many lesbians have found the courage to come out and enjoy the networking, social support, and activities sponsored within this informal community. Activities include book clubs, dance classes, AA, and other support group meetings. There is a strong sense of mutual caring. One oft-repeated dream in the lesbian community is an "old dykes' home."

In 1987, the first Old Lesbians Conference was held in California. They continue their work through the organization Old Lesbians Organizing for Change (OLOC). This group is "committed to networking among old lesbians everywhere in order to confront ageism and heterosexism, develop and disseminate educational materials, facilitate the formation of new groups confronting ageism, and increase visibility for old lesbians within the national women's movement."

Housing is one of the many issues that this group has begun to address.

Since the early nineties Lesbian Natural Resources has supported lesbian community land projects. Their purpose is "to assist Lesbians in obtaining and maintaining community land, in developing rural skills and self-sufficiency, and in community development for Lesbians of many different abilities, ages, races, classes, and economic backgrounds. The intention is to support the growth of Lesbian communities which are actively creating Lesbian culture, preserving land-based life skills and rural ecosystems, and discovering non-oppressive ways to live and work together." This foundation helps groups to develop the skills to build community, and to become a non-profit or Community Land Trust. They have funded projects for land development, purchase of land, and building construction. They support an apprenticeship program, skill bank, resource list, library, and lesbian land archives. The fund accepts donations to continue their work. I hope that someday there are similar funds for other types of women's community projects.

Maize: A Lesbian Country Magazine includes stories and articles about community living. It includes updates on the activities and progress of various groups.

Recently, Shewolf created a "chat room" on the Internet for women interested in developing an intentional community. I like the idea of using a chat room to help women network as they build community; it's useful to all women interested in creating community.

Key Characteristics of Women's Land Communities

- *Structures*—One or more buildings, no common design features.
- *Size*—Generally small, 3 to 5 women but some are larger.
- *Location*—Most rural.
- *Cost*—Varies, generally low.
- *Availability*—Approximately 75 in U.S.
- *Support Services*—Varies on an individual basis. Ask about your interests.
- *Guidelines*—May or may not exist. Ask.
- *Legal*—Cooperative, non-profit, partnership agreements.
- *Special Features*—Generally lesbian organized; some now focusing on aging women; great resource for women's experience in community.

- *Special Concerns*—Lack of written guidelines in some groups; may be economically difficult situations.

One last model of community living remains to be explored here: mobile communities. If you love to travel and hope to incorporate this into your life, perhaps you'll find some ideas that inspire you in the next chapter.

REFERENCES

Barbara Macdonald with Cynthia Rice, *Look Me in the Eye: Old Women Aging and Ageism, Expanded Edition*. San Francisco: Spinsters Book Co., 1991.

Joyce Cheney, *Lesbian Land*. Minneapolis: Word Weaver, 1985.

Lesbian Natural Resources, P.O. Box 8742, Minneapolis, MN 55408.

Maize: A Lesbian Country Magazine, P.O. Box 130, Serafina, NM 87569.

Old Lesbians Organizing for Change, P.O. Box 980422, Houston, TX 77098.

Shewolf, *Directory of Wimmin's Lands*, 2nd ed., New Orleans: Royal T. Pub., 1997.
E-mail: shewolf@nternet.com.
Chat room: shewolfWW@aol.com

CHAPTER 7

RV Living

At one of the workshops I conducted on shared living, a participant described an interesting example of collaborative living. She had been traveling in southern France and found a purse. Following several sets of directions, she arrived at the owner's home—a houseboat in a bay surrounded by other houseboats of friends, a floating community. In the U.S., however, houseboats are expensive, but we do have some other mobile options.

Living on the road is attractive to more and more women. A recreational vehicle (RV) offers a great way to travel alone yet be with other women. Zoe Swanagon and Loverne King founded the organization RVing Women to support this growing interest. The publication *RVing Women Magazine* features articles on topics such as "Tips on Winter Driving," "Bird Watching Sites," and "How to Get Your Mail While on the Road." The group also coordinates RV rallies and caravans. Recent events and activities included a trip to Branson, Missouri, with scheduled entertainment, a raft trip in California, the Balloon Fiesta in Albuquerque,

New Mexico, and a trip through Copper Canyon, Mexico. Knowledge and safety are important to the women and toward this end the group offers frequent RV maintenance events.

When not on the road, an RV needs a home. We've all seen them parked beside a house. However, many RVers live in their vehicles year round in parks designed for the vehicles. To this end, Zoe and Lovern started a private women's RV resort near Phoenix, Arizona, called Pueblo Resort; Discovery Bay and Superstition Mountain were later designed with the same intent. The residents now own these communities. Typically each location has a community center and recreational facilities with scheduled activities such as bridge parties or picnics that offer the residents an opportunity to socialize.

I know one woman who had cardiac surgery while living at Pueblo Resort. Word of her health crisis went out through the large network of RV women who then responded with meals, daily assistance, and emotional support through her recovery.

These resorts are generally in wonderful locations, both urban or rural. They vary in size. Their typical legal structure is condominium or cooperative. An RV is expensive, but used RVs are available. In addition to the cost of the vehicle, community fees must be paid.

Most people need a car in addition to an RV. Nevertheless, many women are attracted to this lifestyle.

Sandra West and Lora Tell, co-owners of Edgewater Resort, an RV campground in California, called to alert me to an interesting, low-cost opportunity for RVers. When they bought the park, it was in need of repair. Then they discovered Workampers, an organization that helps RVers connect with parks that need workers. For a free space and a small salary, workampers do the necessary jobs of park construction, landscaping or routine clean-up. Each park determines their contract with a workamper. Sandra said that they could not have developed or maintained their park without this assistance. Half-joking she said, "I imagine that some day the whole park will have former workampers as year round residents. They're the best friends we have."

Mobile home and manufactured housing communities for women are also being formed. While an RV is designed primarily for traveling, a mobile home is installed in a relatively permanent residential site. A manufactured home is a prefabricated house that is put together in sections. There are newer resorts designed to include all three. My friend Julie bought a vacation home in The Resort on Carefree Boulevard in Ft. Myers, Florida. "When the mountains in New Mexico are snowed in," she said, "I can go to the warmth of the south." There is a clubhouse, walking trail, a hot tub, and other recreational facilities. Recently, older mobile home parks are being converted into cooperatives, some of which are designed for women. Like other co-ops, these locations focus on stabilizing costs as well as developing a sense of community.

Key Characteristics of RV Communities

- *Structures*—Individuals own their own RV and rent, lease, or purchase space in communities; community centers and other facilities are available.
- *Size*—Varies, 15 to 60 units.
- *Location*—Urban or rural near cities.
- *Cost*—Varies.
- *Availability*—RV communities are readily available; women's only locations are now developing.
- *Support Services*—Available on an individual basis, often rely on city services. Ask about the services you want.
- *Guidelines*—May or may not be available.

- *Legal*—Condominium or co-operative structure.
- *Special Features*—Travel opportunities; women's RV communities are a recent development.
- *Special Concerns*—Generally no commitment to care needs as we age; can be expensive.

WOMEN'S RETREATS

Women's camping and retreat centers offer an opportunity to participate in women's community while traveling. Intouch, with over 100 acres, hosts events such as the Women's Over 60 Weekend. Some of the women's communities, such as the Susan B. Anthony Memorial Unrest Home and Owl, offer camping opportunities. While camping out does not provide a home or permanent community, women who want to travel with their friends may find this a women-friendly way to be together in the outdoors.

A mobile lifestyle also may mean sharing homes in various locations. Several women I know each want a home in different locations—travel to home in the mountains, by the water, and in an urban area; they will travel to visit each other in each location part of the year. To make this really work, you'd need to establish a support system of friends, activities and professional help, such as doctors, in all locations; you might even want to have a bank in each community. The idea appeals to me. I've moved to Hawai'i but would like to visit friends in Santa Fe; and they could visit me here in turn.

Women's retreat centers offer community away from home. They are a resource for reflection and rejuvenation. The Holo Center is a nondenominational, new thought ministry. The owners, Julie Keene and Ione Jensen, offer individual sessions using dream therapy, meditation, massages, Gestalt, and other therapeutic activities during scheduled retreats. For fun there's a pool, hot tub, and acres of land. Their book, *Women Alone: Creating a Joyous and Fulfilling Life*, is useful.

Directories, such as the *Communities Directory* and the *Directory of Wimmin's Lands*, are wonderful resources for information. *RVing Women Magazine* also lists many resources for women on the road. My visits to these centers have been wonderful. If you're not committed to participating in a full-time women's community, these camping and retreat centers are a great way to share in women's community.

The next few chapters will discuss issues such as group development and communication skills. There are practical matters, like money. Your vision, discussions with the women in your circle of support, and decisions in these areas will assist you to develop a household of equal partnership with others.

REFERENCES

Julie Keene & Ione Jensen, *Women Alone: Creating a Joyous and Fulfilling Life*. Carson, CA: Hay House, Inc., 1995. To contact the Holo Center, write: E. 955 Grand Tour Dr., Hayden, Idaho 83835. Phone: 208-722-2816. E-mail: holo@nidlink.com

RVing Women Magazine, available through membership in: RVing Women, P.O. Box 1940, Apache Junction, AZ 85127. E-mail: rvingwomen@juno.com

Workamper News, 201 Hiram Road, Heber Springs, AR 72543-8747. E-mail: workamp@arkansas.net. Web site: http://www.workamper.com

CHAPTER 8

Group Development

Your group will go through several phases on its way to creating community. Think back on any relationship or group that you have participated in for any length of time. All those relationships changed over time; if not, they became stagnant. All relationships and groups go through similar phases and decision making and conflict resolution skills are fundamental to the process.

I first learned about these phases of group development while studying to become a group therapist; later I began to see these stages in all my relationships. These phases are like the seasons and cycles in nature, repeating themselves endlessly.

Spring, the time of planning and planting seeds, symbolizes the beginning of any group, the time of hopeful anticipation. Visualization exercises, individual and group assessments regarding intentions, needs, strengths, and challenges are the proper activities of this phase. During this time you will be gathering information and choosing the type of household or community you prefer. You will begin considering appropriate financial agreements, decision making and conflict resolution styles. As you do so, you will come to know yourself and others as potential community members, and you will be developing trust and openness with each other. The first leaders within your group will emerge. Your relationships may seem blissful and idyllic. Enjoy this time because it will not and should not last, just as the falling in love stage does not last. Good communication skills and honesty are fundamental tools. The choices you make and skills you develop during this phase are very important. Your hopes and dreams will be the foundation for future activities of your group.

Summer represents the work phase. The search for a house or land will signal the onset of this phase. Your practical knowledge will increase about concerns like zoning ordinances and taxes. Personal skills such as listening and assertiveness will deepen. Relationships will change. Group members will, hopefully, begin to express their needs more fully; agreements and disagreements will become more apparent. Power will ebb and flow from one person to another; you can view this either as a power struggle or a creative process testing the strength of all. If differences don't emerge, you can assume that they are going underground and will disrupt your work later. With union of the group as your abiding goal, you can view the difficult times as directing your attention to patches of your garden that you may have neglected, or where unseen fruit is waiting to be picked. New levels of leadership will evolve as the needs of the group change and individual talents become apparent. This is a wonderful time for personal and communal learning and growth in many areas and on many levels. Every task completed, each conflict resolved, strengthens your group. Do find time for fun. There is cause for celebration as your dreams of community begin to materialize, just as the seeds in your garden become healthy plants absorbing the sunlight, moisture, and nutrients before they ripen.

One morning you'll sense that "this *is* community"; your efforts will have paid off and many of your dreams will be realized. You will have a collaborative shared living situation with the support, safety, and companionship that you desire. This is the autumn of your group. As you harvest the fruits of your labor, remember to continue the care you provided during previous phases. Differences will continue to emerge, but with the knowledge of previously resolved conflicts you will be able to approach these with increasing creativity and confidence. The outside world may present you with new challenges—the roof may leak or someone may fall ill and need care. During this time you may plant cool weather crops; that is, you may plan for the future while enjoying the present.

Ultimately there is an end to the cycle, the winter. Your community may not "die" but significant changes will occur. Many circumstances may herald this transformation. Just when everything is running smoothly, increasing taxes or decreasing incomes may upset the group's financial stability. Someone may move; someone may die. A dormant time may be necessary to say goodbye and grieve before you can rebuild for the future. Then you will need to renew the group balance and spirit. Surely as the sun comes up every morning, the spring will come again and so will your inspiration to continue your household or community in a new way.

In *Dreaming Down the Dark*, Starhawk likens group development to the four elements. These descriptions emphasize the natural course of phases. Building community requires a lot of work just as any garden requires work, but the rewards are worth it. In the course of your work the essential nature or animating force, the spirit, of your household will emerge. You will find that your shared household, like your garden, will nourish you for years to come.

GROUP ACTIVITIES

The decision to live collaboratively as we age brings us many opportunities for transforming ourselves and our ways of relating to others. We can enter a new life within our shared households or communities. Crafting the spirit of your household is more than the planning, decisions, guidelines, and the model you choose; it exists in the elusive experience of community, in the bonds that hold and enfold your group. Both the intention to create a close household as well as the specific activities to build this unity are important.

One ritual that will honor your commitment to shared living is a house blessing. Once you have settled into your home, consider having some observance of this momentous occasion and all the work it took to get to this point. Rituals solidify the bonds of a group. There are many books about ritual that can help you to develop a blessing, or you may know someone who can help you to create it. This is a time of celebration!

Sharing meals together is a powerful act towards building the spirit of your household. Whether you cook communally or for one another, the act of eating together is both symbolic and practical in creating community. Breaking bread together during hard times can ease the uncomfortable feelings of a conflict or tough decision. You may want to share meals daily or weekly as well as on special occasions.

An increasing number of women are coming together because they sense the importance of spirituality in their daily lives. Shared values and the rituals that express them will help shape the spirit of your household. Your group might do Tai Chi, create a meditation space, light candles before meals, or celebrate spiritual or religious occasions together. Laughter and humor are essential at all times, but particularly when there are difficulties. Cultivate your lighthearted nature. Real community calls for the mind-body-spirit involvement of its members.

While shared living is important, it cannot be everything in your life. Most of the women I talked to who live in community reported that they needed a support system outside their household. A therapist or other counselor may help you work through difficult conflicts. Outside friends are important sources of feedback, helping you gain perspective during times of tension. Know, however, that they may not be objective—after all, they are your friends. Don't underestimate the importance of playmates, someone to meet at the movies, join for a daily walk, a class, or vacation. As we age, we need to work harder to expand our social life or it will naturally contract. The nourishment that you experience outside your household will in turn feed and support your shared living situation.

In the spirit of your household you may find a little mystery and wonder, surprise and delight. Cherish this. At the same time, be aware that community does not happen by mere magic. Difficulties and ruptures in relationships can occur. The next chapter will consider some of the specific skills that, when implemented, will help your household through these times to become the supportive circle that you envision for your elder years.

REFERENCES

Corinne McLaughlin and Gordon Davidson, *Dawn: Community Lifestyles in a Changing World*. Summertown, TN: Book Publishing Co., 1985.

Carolyn R. Shaffer and Kristin Anundsen, *Creating Community Anywhere: Finding Support and Connection in a Fragmented World*. New York: Jeremy P. Tarcher, 1993.

Starhawk, *Dreaming the Dark: Magic, Sex and Politics*. Boston: Beacon Press, 1982.

Claude Whitmyer, ed. *In the Company of Others: Making Community in the Modern World*. New York: Jeremy P. Tarcher, 1993.

CHAPTER 9

Skills Needed for Living in Community

There are specific skills that will help you face the challenges of living together. Decision making and conflict resolution skills are fundamental to strong, healthy relationships. As a psychotherapist I've spent considerable time teaching people how to solve problems. I believe that the ideas presented here will help your group. Please reflect on what you've already learned in past experiences and rely on that knowledge as well. It is fundamental that you come from a heart-felt place of compassion and respect in your interactions with those with whom you live. With self-awareness, care, and skill you will be working with heart in your household.

MAKING DECISIONS

Any household or community, like any relationship, needs to make decisions. Your group will need to give thought and attention to the means of decision making. The ways in which you share power can contribute to the bonds of closeness in your household, or they can create dissension and divisiveness.

Most of us are familiar with top down decision making. When we were children, our parents made decisions for us. In the best scenario we saw them jointly make these decisions, but more often than not, one parent held most of the power. In our larger society, men generally hold much of the power. Most of us have had numerous personal and work experiences in which men have been the decision makers. Increasingly, however, women have created situations where we have had the power to make decisions, though this, too, may have been in a hierarchical—power-over—context. In an effort to develop more egalitarian relationships, methods of shared decision making, such as voting or majority rule, have evolved. You may find that these approaches have their time and place in your community.

Spreading from its roots in the Native American and Quaker communities, consensus decision making is growing in popularity. Collective decision making produces high-quality solutions because of the value placed on each person's views and the exploration of individual needs and differences. Responsibility and accountability increase for each person and for the group. Cooperation enhances self-esteem and creativity. Building consensus is a process that honors the power of the whole group. Consensus is important as a method of considering issues as well as a method for arriving at decisions. I believe consensus decision making has great potential to contribute to strong, healthy, shared living situations.

As women we have often been discouraged from participating in decision making. We may have found it difficult to speak up, develop, and use our personal power. Using the techniques of consensus building, we can learn to voice our concerns and objections. We can develop the ability to press on when necessary. We can also understand, after we have been heard, that it may be exploitive to ask the group to change for our individual needs. We can learn to find the balance between individual and group needs.

In one workshop a woman said, "For two years I was in a group that used consensus decision making and we never made even one decision because we could never all agree." This statement reflects a commonly held misconception about consensus decision making—that everyone must agree. In practice, consensus is a state of mutual agreement in which participants hear all legitimate concerns. This does not, however, mean that there is total agreement on everything by everyone. The consensus process is designed to accommodate differences of opinion. You may not want to use consensus for all decisions, however; some decisions that seem minor would take more time to discuss than their impact warrants. Your group will need to decide when and where consensus best satisfies your needs.

Consensus building can follow a formal process or be spontaneous; it is dynamic. You can adapt it to suit the needs of your group at various times and phases of development. A facilitator guides the group through the stages of decision making, but does not vote on that issue. Ideally the role of group facilitator rotates over time so that everyone can participate in the decision making as well as develop the ability to guide the group. As with any decision-making method, a recorder or secretary will be necessary.

In the full process of building consensus, the following stages occur:

- *Ideas and concerns emerge.*
- *A proposal is presented.*
  These may circulate among the members ahead of the meeting so that everyone can come to the discussion with thoughts and questions. Concerns about the proposal are posed and clarified.

- *A group discussion follows.*
  Concerns and points of agreement emerge during this stage. All matters need to be fully heard and understood. The proposal may be modified as new information is gained. After being heard, members with concerns may choose to "stand aside." This position signals, "My concerns have been heard. I do not agree with the proposal, but I will not get in the way of this decision." These members may also choose not to participate in carrying out the proposal and should indicate this.
- *Ultimately, concerns are resolved.*
  A deeper consideration of the expressed concerns may be necessary; this should be done one matter at a time. The proposed solution may be reviewed in relation to the group's purpose and values. The motives underlying the proposed solution or the concerns may be considered. During this stage concerns may be resolved, new and better solutions may emerge, or members may come to a place of being able to stand aside so that consensus can be reached. Ultimately,

there is a vote indicating agreement and support or a stand aside position. If the majority of the group disagrees with the proposal, that would have become apparent during the discussion and the vote would be against the proposal. Thus, consensus is achieved.

- *Options close.*
  If the work of the above stages does not result in consensus either for or against a proposal, there still needs to be closure. Subgroups or committees may be formed to gather more information and return later. The group may not be ready to function by consensus, indicating a need for increased formal and informal trust-building activities. A "block" may be declared if the group cannot reach consensus. Some groups use a "super majority" vote, that is, 66 to 90 percent agreement to make decisions when consensus cannot be achieved. The use of this "fallback position" needs to be articulated ahead of time and used judiciously so as not to undermine the process of consensus building. The group may choose to go

into a conflict resolution phase as will be discussed in the next section of this chapter.

Maturity, flexibility, and a willingness to work in a group are necessary to the use of consensus decision making. Caring for one another will strengthen your decision making process. This method takes more time than the hierarchical or majority rule varieties of decision making. The group needs to be willing to give time to learn and use the process of consensus. In so doing, I believe that this method will lead to good group decisions and strong bonds of community.

Learning to participate in a consensus process has been a challenge for me. I tend to talk a lot; I want things decided quickly. My challenge has been to develop patience. So, I'm learning to sit quietly as all participants speak and the group discusses its concerns. This has helped me to pay attention to the process as much as the specifics of the discussion. In this way I can see decisions evolving. This process has contributed to creating a strong group with a high level of trust and respect. The high quality of group decisions has led to productive outcomes in line with the group's purpose.

CONFLICT RESOLUTION

Conflict means to "meet with differences." Both the "meeting" and the "differences" are integral. We all see things differently, and have different needs, experiences, and styles. Disagreements arise when someone says or does something that challenges another person's world view. Such a challenge requires us to think in new ways and find resolutions that take into account others' experiences and perspectives.

Conflict resolution is the means by which individuals seek common ground, transforming their differing views into something new that is hopefully better for all. When addressed openly, conflicts can lead to better understanding, stronger relationships, and creative problem solving. When conflict is mishandled or not addressed, resentments can build that will destroy relationships or your community. Before the occasion arises, an agreement to address conflicts as soon as possible and to use an agreed-on method of doing so will help you to move through these times more easily. To feel safe, agree to nonviolence, in deed *and* word. Describe behavior, but don't attempt to interpret another's intent, and don't blame anyone. I recommend that you also use a "time out" of a predetermined length when problems are too intense. When you declare a "time out" you are saying that just now you can't go on any further; you need a time apart to calm down and reflect. Then you can come back to address the problem. A willingness to tell the truth, to be authentic, and to accept change are fundamental to all efforts at conflict resolution.

Differences in power and threats of violence make it very difficult to create solutions. When only one person is working from a place of integrity, genuine resolutions are impossible. For the most part, I utilize the best skills I know to address differences and conflicts when they arise. Personally, I tend to avoid situations where sincere resolutions are unlikely, while others take them on as an opportunity to effect change. I suspect that in the long run, both approaches are needed.

The quality of our thoughts is a tremendous asset, or liability, in this process. Not only what we think, but how we think—whether our thoughts come from depression or from well-being—affects our interactions with others. When we are in a low mood where all is not right in the world, our thoughts and our resulting feelings are colored by this mood. When we are coming from a place of well-being, of gratitude and even inspiration, our thoughts and feelings are more trustworthy. A low mood is not conducive to addressing differences. Fortunately, our moods change all the time. Learn to watch your moods, and the resulting effects they have on the quality of your thoughts and feelings. Wait for a sense of well-being and compassion before you approach others with whom you have differences. In so doing, you will more readily find the wisdom of new, helpful solutions within you.

When differences lead to conflicts, various feelings can emerge—confusion, anger, hurt, fear, guilt, and shame. These feelings can propel us back to other times of conflict in our lives, particularly childhood. The feelings from those earlier situations can mesh with our present feelings and create considerable intensity. Ah, here it is again, a time to become aware of the habitual thought patterns that lead to these feelings. Those recurring thoughts and feelings are not a statement about us or our ability to deal with our issues. Their emergence is a statement about life—we tend to get caught up in old thoughts and feelings. Conflict will happen and growth opportunities will appear. Recognizing these old patterns, these old movies, can be your first ally to help you move beyond them to address the current conflict appropriately. Keep in mind that the person with whom you are in conflict probably has a similar pool of old, often overwhelming, thoughts and feelings. Consider:

- What low mood and old thought patterns are occurring within you?
- How is this situation like something in the past?
- How is this situation different from one in the past? How are you different today from the person you were in the past?
- How might you think differently in this situation today? As you think these new thoughts, how do your feelings change? What choices or options for action do you have available to you today that you didn't in the past?

During disagreements, I always need to remember that I'm not a child anymore; the person I'm dealing with is not my parent who has all the power. Keeping this in mind helps me to move beyond some of my ingrained thoughts and feelings. I encourage you to have compassion for yourself and others at times like these.

If you're in a low mood, or your mood drops as you talk, wait for your mood and thoughts to lift before continuing. You can facilitate this shift by relinquishing your grip on the problem at hand and focusing on something else, something uplifting or a time when you were able to move through a conflict with ease. Most likely your mood will improve and you can address the concerns more productively. When you are discussing differences, please listen and attempt to truly get one another's perspective, thoughts, and feelings. Don't listen in a surface way while you are planning your tactics. Listen with an attitude of loving the person speaking. If you practice open-hearted listening and other principles of good communication, it will become easier to implement these skills during times of distress.

As you consider a specific conflict, reflect on your group's stage of development. Ask yourself how your particular disagreement may be part of the group's growing pains. Growing pains are an opportunity for growth. Your individual needs and actions flow from and back to those of the whole group. Some of the early conflicts in a group arise out of the newness of the relationships, uncertain roles and commitments. Later conflicts can relate to the core of one's beliefs and behavior, presenting a tremendous opportunity for personal and group change and growth. In moments of such reflection you can gain important insights.

After you describe the problem, how you think *you* got there, and how you think it affects you, it is imperative that you move on to discussing possible solutions and building them. Search for a resolution that reflects the highest level of health, well-being, and good for all. In so doing, ask yourself these questions:

- If a miracle happened and this disagreement were resolved, what would the solution look like?
- How will you know that you have resolved this conflict?
- When you reach a resolution, what will you be thinking and feeling? What will you be doing? What will others be doing?
- In the past, how have you successfully handled similar problems?
- What would give you and others the knowledge that you have arrived at a reconciliation?
- When did you already think, feel, and act in ways that were part of the solution? What will make those times likely to occur more often?

Solutions need to be specific. Find out who will do what, when, where, and how. Record and date the agreed upon solution for future reference. The next step is action, putting your solution into place. You can recognize a solution when you carry it out and it helps everybody. At those times, you and others will have a sense of well-being and intimacy. After implementing a solution, get together again to evaluate its effectiveness. You can make changes as they are needed.

Many cultures use a "talking stick" to honor a speaker and encourage everyone to listen. Some communities meditate together, asking for clarity and guidance before and during times of conflict resolution. One women's group uses singing as a means of shifting the energy in the group during times of conflict. Other devices may be helpful to you.

Sometimes it may be useful to have someone neutral or objective to help you build solutions. This person can function in many ways. She can be a translator, helping you hear each other. She can be a fair witness, sitting with you, observing your process, and holding the space for your resolution within her heart. She can arbitrate, listen to both sides and present a solution that you have agreed to accept in advance. She can be a mediator, helping you develop your own solutions. Someone within the household can fill these roles or you may call in someone from the outside.

During conflicts it is sometimes difficult to keep your spirits up, even when positive outcomes are assured. Often there are no quick results. These times call for patience and perseverance. Please remember the people and activities that replenish and sustain you. Much as partners or parents and children hug following a disagreement, the members of your household will also need to find ways of rejoining. The activities of daily living—pulling weeds, sharing a meal, lighting candles—may help to ease hurt feelings. Group laughter, hugs, or cleansing rituals may be useful. This is also part of building and sustaining healthy relationships.

These skills of decision making and conflict resolution will help you to build a strong shared living household. When implemented from your heart they will help your community to move more smoothly through making decisions and dealing with disagreements. They are not, however, the only skills you will need. Practical matters need your attention as well. The next chapter will consider some of these other concerns.

REFERENCES

Michel Avery, Brian Auvine, Barbara Streibel, and Lonnie Weiss, *Building United Judgment: A Handbook for Consensus Decision Making*. Madison, WI: Center for Conflict Resolution, 1981. The center has many other fine resources on this topic.

Steven Saint and James R. Lawson, *Rules for Reaching Consensus: A Modern Approach to Decision Making*. San Diego: Pfeiffer & Co., 1994.

Starhawk, *Truth or Dare: Encounters with Power, Authority and Mystery*. San Francisco: Harper and Row, Publishers, 1987.

CHAPTER 10

Women and Money

For many years I cringed when I considered financial and legal matters. I knew it was in my best interest to make sense of money matters, but I resisted for a long time. When I got divorced, I changed. Slowly, sometimes unwillingly, I came to understand money and legal affairs. It's an ongoing, never-ending learning process. Since I knew I had to be more responsible if I was going to live with friends, I have learned. So can you.

Consider these factors which affect a woman's financial circumstances:

- Women typically have lower-paying jobs than men.
- Women move in and out of jobs more frequently than men because we tend to follow the careers of partners and assume the full-time care for children and aging relatives.
- Single-parent households are typically headed by women. Thus the demands on a woman's income are often great.

- Divorce rates are high, leaving women single.
- Women outlive men.
- Most women are not eligible for pension benefits.
- Until recently, pre-retirement planning was primarily designed for and offered to men.

Is it any wonder that we have difficulty making financial plans? By talking with other women about money, you can relax about your lack of knowledge. You can ask questions again and again, or hear similar confusion around you. Slowly you can begin to understand the concepts that underlie economics and gain confidence.

I encourage you to address your concerns regarding money matters in two ways: attitudinally and behaviorally. Believing that you cannot successfully manage your money or that you cannot earn enough to save for the future will create this reality. Please look at your thoughts and beliefs about money. Do they empower you? If not, change them; this is not simple, but is fundamental. Identify specifically what you tell yourself about money. Replace any negative thought about your skills handling money with a more positive one. This may be a matter of forced thought at first, but it will help. Your thoughts, in and of themselves, are very powerful. If you do this work of changing your beliefs within a group of women, they can offer encouragement and support.

As your thoughts, beliefs, and attitudes shift, so will your behavior. In one group a friend suggested never making a cash purchase using coins. Rather, she said, "Use only dollar bills—take the small change and save it." I did it for a month and saved $21.00. It was relatively painless. I pass this idea on to you. Changing your behavior in many small ways will add up.

All financial planning experts suggest that you set clear financial goals that are in line with your values, lifestyle, and dreams. Undoubtedly this will include some goals about the money you will need in retirement. Next you'll need to determine how you're doing towards meeting those goals. Begin by tracking all your expenses and spending for a month and compare this with your income. Does your accounting indicate that you're achieving the goals that you have set for yourself? If not, you'll need to change your spending, earning, and savings habits. If you're significantly in debt, locate the Consumer Credit Counseling Service, or other similar business in your area. This group can help you sort through these difficulties and plan a strategy for getting out of debt.

There are many good books available on money management, retirement planning, Social Security, and related topics. Try spending an evening in the personal finance section of your local library or a good bookstore. (Then, if you're a wise shopper, you'll borrow the book you like best from your local library or through interlibrary loan.) A simple pamphlet that I recommend is *Social Security... What Every Woman Should Know*, published by the Social Security Administration. The National Center for Women and Retirement Research has produced a good workbook, Pre-Retirement Education Planning Program for Women (PREP), and conducts workshops that are designed to assist women in financial planning as we age. Community colleges and service organizations often give seminars on financial planning.

Savings accounts and Certificates of Deposit, which pay relatively low interest, are safe investments—but really only a little better than cookie jars. What's the alternative? Stocks and bonds? Until a few years ago the stock market bewildered and frightened me. Also, I considered it part of the big boys' game, and wanted none of it. Then I heard about the Beardstown ladies and other women's investment clubs, and when I learned that women's investment groups often outperform men's clubs, I took notice. "There's something here," I thought, "a woman's way of investing."

Investment clubs have been around for many years. Individuals come together to learn about sound investing. They pool money and invest. Their financial goals typically include long-term investing. The Beardstown ladies suggest having fun and eating together at meetings as well. The National Association of Investors Corporation (NAIC) is an excellent resource for support if you hope to start such a group.

Studies indicate that since women have always done the shopping in a household, they surely are able to make good investment choices. Moreover, as women we listen to one another. It's sound reasoning to join a club, if merely for the fun of it.

In January of 1996, I started an investment club with twelve women, named the Crone's Nest Egg. For the next eighteen months we met once a month over pot luck dinners. We developed a consensus regarding our financial goals and bylaws. We began learning financial principles. In the spring of 1997 the group made its first two purchases; it was a night of celebration! When I moved and was no longer able to attend the club, I asked the members for comments, because I knew I'd probably start or join another investment group. Members reported that they were thankful for the opportunity to learn about finance in a safe, supportive environment; they felt more confident regarding their abilities, and they'd begun the process of wise, long-term investing.

I encourage you to consider joining or starting a women's investment club. We began with a personal investment of $25.00 a month; later we increased that amount. Even a group of ten women investing $5.00 per month will accumulate a sizable amount over time. In the active stock market of the past few years, baby boomers and women specifically are investing in increasing numbers.

ECONOMIC CONSIDERATIONS AND SHARED HOUSING

In your old age, what will you be able to afford? The recommendation is that your housing costs be no more than 1/3 your income. Remember, your income will be less as you age. However, by living collaboratively, you and others are better equipped. Consider these questions:

- What will be the source of your money—savings, Social Security, employment?

- If you live in a rural area, how will you earn money?
- Will you develop a cottage industry? How long will that take before it can support you?
- Will you need to support yourself until your household or community becomes self-sustaining? If so, will you commute to a city to work?

You will need to consider many issues and reach agreement regarding how you will handle shared economic concerns.

- Beyond the mortgage payments, will there be a community fee to pay for shared needs such as a new washing machine or repairs to the house? Will you personally save for these community needs?
- If the income or resources of the women in your group are considerably different from yours, will that matter? How?
- When renting or buying a home, will you invest equally or in proportion to your financial resources?

- Are there other ways that someone might invest in your household? What about sweat, skill, or service equity? For example, if one of you did all the legal and real estate negotiations for the purchase, would that count as part of a down payment?
- What if you remodel an older home while your friend buys the materials; is that an equal exchange?
- What if one person does all the household cooking and cleaning; would that have a financial value?
- Can you imagine a household economy based on "gifting" versus an exchange of money or work? For a wonderful resource for further information, read Genevieve Vaughan's book, *For-Giving*.

You will need to consider whether to reserve money for personal emergencies such as increased taxes or medical expenses.

- How will you handle such crises?
- How will the community respond to unexpected illness or decreased functioning?

What if these changes affect a member's ability to keep financial commitments?

- If one member needs care and another provides it, would the financial arrangement change?
- How would one woman's changing capacities and financial resources affect the interpersonal relationships within the group?
- If one woman leaves the community, how would you establish her equity? Could she sell her portion outright? Must the group approve the new buyer?
- And if she dies, does her property go to her heirs or back to the community?

You will need to and agree about these matters ahead of time to help you avoid conflicts. The answers will lead you to the particular legal structure that is most appropriate for your group.

FINANCING A COLLABORATIVE LIVING SITUATION

When your plans include a shared purchase, traditional lending institutions will consider your financial stability, income, and the down payment that you are able to make. Here again, pooling your resources will improve your chances. Local lending institutions are the most common resource for funding, even for shared housing. Lenders, property owners, and the future residents become involved in a shared project. You can enhance your ability to secure traditional funding if you or some member of your group already have a relationship with an officer in a lending institution. A consultant or lawyer who has experience with the financing of cooperative ventures will also be very helpful.

The federal government, through the Affordable Housing Act of 1990, has taken a new interest in non-traditional housing options, particularly affordable housing options. According to the requirements of the Community Reinvestment Act, banks must allocate a certain percentage of their loan activity for affordable housing and other socially responsible activities. Your project may fit these requirements. The Federal Home Loan Bank has an Affordable Housing Program that might also be a resource to you. The Center for Cooperative Housing, a subsidiary of the National Association of Housing Cooperatives (NAHC), will provide technical assistance to those interested in federal funds for housing cooperatives. The director of NAHC, Herbert Cooper-Levy, is a good resource; when I contacted him about this book, he sent me several interesting articles. You will find that by joining this organization or others, you will be connected with people who have a similar vision. Their knowledge and experience may be very valuable.

State and local resources for financing change frequently and vary according to location. However, community development block grant funds, redevelopment housing funds, tax credits, and other special programs are worth investigating. Contact your local non-profit housing development organizations for information about local resources.

There are some resources available specifically for collaborative housing ventures. The National Association of Community Development Loan Funds (NACDLF) is a federation of community groups that provides financing for housing cooperatives and community land trusts, particularly to low- and middle-income individuals. Contact the National Cooperative Bank (NCB) if you plan a co-op. They can assist with funding to develop, purchase, construct, rehabilitate, or refinance cooperatively owned real estate. An affiliate of the NCB, the NCB Development Corporation, focuses on low-income cooperative housing. The NCB Savings Association is a resource for share loans to buy a share in a cooperative.

You might investigate the resources of a private lending pool. Members of such a pool contribute money exclusively for housing funding. A private offering is a legal partnership or joint venture between the pool participants and the housing group. Friends or other interested individuals with resources to allocate for such an activity can comprise the pool. These investors may welcome the opportunity to contribute to the creation of a women's household or community.

Another possible method of financing your household is an equity sharing arrangement where the lender provides the funds for a down payment and co-owns the property. The lender thereby gets a relatively trouble-free investment and tax advantages. The other co-owner/occupant gets help acquiring a home and the tax advantages of home ownership. Mortgage payments are paid by the occupant. Both parties agree to share the future appreciation of the property. There are laws and restrictions that protect both parties in equity-sharing arrangements. Again, you will need to contact an experienced lawyer to help you with this method of ownership.

In traditional loans you have a mortgage held by a lending institution. If you develop an alternative financial arrangement, however personal and private, do make these agreements legal. Some women who have not had written contracts discovered that their verbal agreements fell apart. They will tell you that there is wisdom in having written agreements. "An agreement is an agreement until it becomes a disagreement," said Susan Turetsky of the Landlord/Tenant Hotline in Santa Fe, New Mexico.

LEGAL STRUCTURES FOR SHARED HOUSING

There are several legal categories of shared ownership. To make wise choices regarding which ownership model and legal structure is most appropriate for you and your household or group, you will want to understand the contractual, tax, inheritance, and resale considerations of each method. As with many options described in this book, there is no "best" way of structuring your household or community. As you become informed, you can choose the model that best suits your vision and needs. Always check with a lawyer to see which method is best for you

- "Joint tenants" are two or more individuals who share property ownership, each owning an undivided interest in the property and each having "right of survivorship." Married couples typically buy property as joint tenants, but any two people can do so. With this method, there is one title to the entire property and ownership is held jointly. Each owner has an equal right to share in the use and enjoyment of the property during their respective lives. When one owner dies, the shared property automatically passes to the surviving owner. If an owner sells her portion, this breaks or severs the joint tenancy agreement and new owners become tenants-in-common, thus defeating the survivorship right of the other joint tenants.

- In contrast, "tenancy-in-common" is the most frequent form of collaborative ownership. Each co-owner has a separate legal title to her undivided interest in the property. In this agreement, owners can pass their ownership interest to their heirs. Owners typically have broad rights to the use of their share; that is, even if holding unequal shares they are each entitled to equal use and possession. They can sell their interest in the property for profit or to satisfy a debt or otherwise dispose of the property. The new owner becomes a tenant-in-common with the former owners.

- In a "partnership," individuals carry on unincorporated business; ownership interest is in proportion to interest in the partnership. No partner can sell her interest without consent of the other partners. At death, the individual's interest in the partnership passes to the surviving partners unless that partnership was liquidated, in which case the interest will go to the heirs, or unless the partnership agreement provides for other disposition of the property.
- In a "cooperative," group members own shares of common assets; these can be sold at the end of membership. In most co-ops, the resale price is restricted by predetermined agreement. The articles of incorporation must provide for open membership, democratic control, political neutrality, and limited return on shares for limited-equity cooperatives. Cooperatives can be for profit

or non-profit.

- A "condominium" combines a title to a housing unit with joint ownership of common elements shared with other unit owners. "Corporations" are legal and taxable entities regulated by state law. They may be for profit or non-profit. There are several different types of corporations that apply to housing ownership.

Each state has unique and specific legal definitions for cooperatives and corporations that include tax, resale, and inheritance implications. As you become familiar with these legal options, you can make choices regarding the ownership model that best reflects your interests.

REFERENCES

Beardstown Ladies Investment Club with Leslie Whitaker, *Beardstown Ladies' Common-Sense Investment Guide: How We Beat the Stock Market—and How You Can, Too*. New York: Hyperion, 1994.

Diana Bull and Elaine St. James, *The Equity Sharing Book: How to Buy a Home Even If You Can't Afford the Down Payment*. New York: Penguin, 1990.

Genevieve Vaughan, *For-Giving*. Austin, TX: Plain View Press, 1997.

"Landlord/Tenant Handbook." I obtained this, along with a copy of the Uniform Owner-Resident Relations Act of New Mexico state law, from the Landlord/Tenant Hotline. I found similar information on the Internet and through the state government when I moved to Hawai'i. To locate a similar service in your community, call the state attorney general or a legal aid organization regarding a tenant advocacy organization.

Lottie Cohen and Lois Arkin, eds. *Cooperative Housing Compendium: Resources for Collaborative Living*. Center for Cooperatives, UC Davis, Davis, CA 95616. This book defines and describes the various models of shared ownership. It outlines interpersonal and financial aspects of each. I highly recommend this resource for a further comparative analysis of community models.

National Association of Community Development Loan Funds, 924 Cherry St., 3rd Floor, Philadelphia, PA 19107. Phone: 215-923-4754

National Association of Housing Cooperatives and The Center for Cooperative Housing, 1614 King Street, Alexandria, VA 22314. Phone: 703-549-5201

National Association of Investors Corporation, 711 W. Thirteen-Mile Road, Madison Heights, MI 48071. Phone: 810-583-6242

National Cooperative Bank and The NBC Development Corporation, 1401 Eye Street NW, Suite 700, Washington, DC 20005. Phone: 202-336-7680

NCB Savings Association, P.O. Box 66p, Hillsboro, OH 45133.

Neale S. Godfrey with Tad Richards, *Making Change: A Woman's Guide to Designing Her Financial Future.* New York: Simon & Schuster, 1977.

Pre-Retirement Education Planning Program for Women (PREP), developed by the National Center for Women and Retirement Research, Long Island University, Southampton Campus, Southampton, NY 11968.

Susan Laubach, *The Whole Kit and Caboodle: A Novel Approach.* Baltimore: Bancroft Press, 1996. This storybook approach presents investment fundamentals in a clear, entertaining format.

Suze Orman, *The Nine Steps to Financial Freedom: Practical and Spiritual Steps So You Can Stop Worrying.* New York: Crown Publishers, 1992.

Suze Orman with Linda Mead, *You've Earned, Don't Lose It: Mistakes You Can't Afford to Make When You Retire*, Revised & updated edition. New York: Newmarket Press, 1997.

Twin Pines Cooperative Foundation, Co-op Resource Center, 1442 A. Walnut Street, Suite 415, Berkeley, CA 94709-1045. Phone: 510-232-1111

U.S. Department of Health and Human Services, Social Security Administration, *Social Security... What Every Woman Should Know*, SSA Publication No. 05-10127, ICN 480067. Phone: 1-800-772-1213, TTY: 1-800-325-0778.

CHAPTER 11

One Vision of Community

I'll tell you one more story about a community of women that I find inspiring.

Imagine—you're living in your home of many years. Three houses down and across the street lives your best friend. Next door lives her sister. One block over lives a woman you used to work with and her partner. In the next block lives her cousin. Five houses away from her live two women who had heard about the women in the neighborhood and wanted to live there too. In all, there are 75 women living in a ten-block area.

Fantasy? No. This scattered-site community actually exists in the Dutch Hill area of Kansas City, Missouri. The group of women now call themselves "Womontown." It was the dream of two women, Andrea and Mary Ann, who bought and restored a house in Dutch Hill. The neighborhood wasn't safe, however, for them or the elderly women already living nearby, and there was no true neighborhood feeling. It was particularly important to them that Womontown be open and supportive to lesbians. Developers were waiting in the wings preparing to move in. Instead of being discouraged, the women decided to build community. Andrea's background as a general contractor and property manager was fundamental. She took a job in government housing programs with the city. Mary Ann, an English professor, technical writer, and feminist, began to contact other women and market their idea of community—a safe place.

Knowing that many women couldn't afford even moderate housing because their work history was sporadic and their incomes low, Andrea and Mary Ann worked with realtors and bankers to make the area women friendly. They began to address their concerns about crime and drug dealing. "With help from many women, we created a May festival, planted tulips to reidentify with Dutch Hill heritage and created a revitalized image of the neighborhood. We got acquainted, planted and cleaned for the elderly. We cleared vacant lots and alleys of trash, encouraged crime walks for unity and courage, called to have street lights repaired and abandoned furniture removed. Together we worked to fix up our homes." They joined the local neighborhood association.

Many single, elderly women were already living in Dutch Hill when Andrea and Mary Ann moved in. Some would peek out behind locked doors whenever anyone approached. Without the skills and energy to keep up their property, their homes were deteriorating. Once Womontown developed, this changed. Andrea tells the story of one elderly woman who became disoriented and walked away from her home. Quickly, neighbors became concerned and began looking for her. At dusk she returned, on the arm of another elderly woman.

The resulting community of women is not a fluke. It could happen anywhere. It begins with two or three committed women who are willing to work hard. They need to have a vision, be willing to become savvy about the system, and be advocates for others. Everyone in the area benefits.

I am fortunate to have connected with so many women when I was writing this book. From many perspectives, urban and rural, small households or large communities, women are showing me that living with friends, creating a Crone's Nest, is enriching, revitalizing, and fun. These women by their endeavors have expanded what is possible for us exponentially.

There is a pressing need at this time to break free of old lifestyle patterns and to craft our futures as we want them to be. If we choose, our efforts can impact not only our households and neighborhoods, but also city, state, and federal government planning, regarding housing for all the elderly. Our strength is in our numbers, our unity, and the collective recognition of our unique needs as we age. As a generation of old women, larger than any generation before us, our power can and will be felt. This is an exciting and powerful opportunity for change that has only just begun. Together we can give birth to a new reality for old women.

REFERENCES

For further information about Womontown, contact:

Andrea Nedelsky and Mary Ann Hopper,
654 Charing Cross Drive, Marietta, GA 30066.
Phone: 1-800-604-3701. E-mail: mhopper@aol.com

CHAPTER 12

Steps to Realizing Your Dreams

This section outlines the major steps and activities that you will undertake as you move towards and into collaborative living. The order presented here is not rigid and you may find that there are activities that are important to you that I have not listed.

STEP ONE

Waking Up

Write down your thoughts and feelings about how you want your elder years to be. Inform yourself about the conditions of women as we age and how these might affect you. Note any preparation you have already done.

STEP TWO

Envisioning Your Elder Years

Identify your dreams for your future as an old woman. Describe your ideal living situation in as much detail as possible.

STEP THREE

Self-assessment

Use the self-assessment tools in this book and elsewhere to help you determine the strengths and difficulties that you bring to collaborative living. Learn new skills in areas where you need to grow so that you will be comfortable and successful in shared living.

STEP FOUR

Creating a Circle of Support

Form a group with other women who want to consciously plan for collaborative living as you age. Together, identify and work through your fears of aging. Begin creating a joint vision of your ideal collaborative living situation. Make a commitment to meet regularly to work towards your vision.

STEP FIVE

Energize Your Vision

Begin group discussions regarding your intention and focus, preferred model of shared living, physical setting and structure for a collaborative lifestyle. Explore possible decision making and problem solving models. Consider the larger neighborhood issues. Gather information about financial and legal concerns. If you haven't already done so, begin saving money towards your retirement. Discuss your wishes and plans when you die. Recognize and discuss your personal, economic, and other limitations. Visit existing shared living households and communities. Write notes on your vision to later weave into group agreements. With your group, engage in social activities to build bonds of community.

STEP SIX

Conscious Planning

Develop group agreements and guidelines regarding membership, preferred housing and organizational structures, ownership models and shared economics. Plan for changes over time. Choose and begin to implement your preferred models of decision making and problem resolution. Hire consultants—financial, legal, construction, etc., as needed.

STEP SEVEN

Pre-Ownership Activities

Investigate and view potential houses, land, communities, etc. Secure down payment and loan funds. If you are building, as opposed to joining an active community or buying an existing property, you will need to engage in a lengthy development phase with architects, contractors, etc. Sign contracts and make purchases. Build or remodel as needed.

STEP EIGHT

Living Your Dreams

Move in! Have a houseblessing and celebration. Enjoy decorating your home. Assume responsibility for bill payment, cleaning, cooking, trash collection, gardening and other yard maintenance activities, household repairs, networking with neighbors, and caregiving as needed. Continue your regular meetings and social gatherings. Make changes as needed.

STEP NINE

Sweet Endings

As we age, we will change. Previous agreements and contracts should dictate legal matters. With your housemates or community members, discuss how these changes are affecting you. Adapt your shared living situation as needed. When group members leave or die, develop rituals to acknowledge these passages.

QUICK REFERENCE TO COMMUNITY RESOURCES

Center for Cooperatives
UC Davis
Davis, CA 95616

Cohousing Network
P.O. Box 2584
Berkeley, CA 94702
Web site:
http://www.cohousing/org

Co-op Resource Center
1442 A Walnut Street, #415
Berkeley, CA 94709

Ecovillage Network of the Americas
P.O. Box 90, The Farm
Summertown, TN 38483-0090
E-mail: ecovillage@thefarm.org

Federation of Egalitarian Communities
138 Twin Oaks Road
Louisa, VA 23093
Phone: 540-894-5126
Web Page: http://www.crl.com/`eastwind/fec/htm
E-mail: FEC@ic.org

Fellowship for Intentional Community
Route 1, Box 155
Rutledge, MO 63563
Web site: http://www.well.com/user/cmty/fic/

Gray Panthers
1424 16th Street, NW
Washington, DC 20036
Phone: 202-387-3111

Holo Center, Women's Retreat
E. 955 Grand Tour Drive
Hayden, ID 83835
Phone: 208-722-2816
E-mail: holo@nidlink.com

Institute for Community Economics
57 School Street
Springfield, MA 01105

Lesbian Natural Resources
P.O. Box 8742
Minneapolis, MN 55408

McGee Foundation
P.O. Box 56756
Washington, DC 20040
E-mail: oegeberg@capacess.org

National Association of Housing Cooperative and Center for Cooperative Housing
1614 King Street
Alexandria, VA 22314

National Center for Women and Retirement Research
Long Island University, Southampton Campus
South Hampton, NY 11968

National Cooperative Bank and The NBC Development Corporation
1401 Eye Street NW, Suite 700
Washington, DC 20005
Phone: 202-336-7680

National Shared Housing Resource Center
431 Pine Street
Burlington, VT 05401
Phone: 1-800-862-2727

Older Woman's League (OWL)
666 11th Street, NW #700
Washington, DC 20001
Phone: 202-783-6686

Old Lesbians Organizing for Change
P.O. Box 980422
Houston, TX 77098

Rving Women
P.O. Box 1940
Apache Junction, AZ 85127
E-mail: rvingwomen@juno.com

Shared Living Resource Center
237 Shattuck Avenue
Berkeley, CA 94704
Phone: 510-548-6608

Shewolf Wimmin's Community Resources
E-mail: shewolf@nternet.com
Chat room: shewolfWW@aol.com

U.S. Department of Health and Human Services Social Security Administration
Phone: 1-800-772-1213
TTY: 1-800-325-0778

Womontown, Andrea Nedelsky and Mary Ann Hopper
654 Charing Cross Drive
Marietta, GA 30066
Phone: 1-800-604-3701
E-mail: mhopper@aol.com

Workampers
201 Hiram Road
Heber Springs, AR 72543-8747
E-mail: workamp@arkansas.net
Web site: http://www.workamper.com

INDEX

Books by The Crossing Press

A Foxy Old Woman's Guide to Traveling Alone

By Jay Ben-Lesser

"A delightful hoot that will appeal to travelers of all ages. Put on your sensible shoes and get ready for a reading treat!"

—*Library Journal*

$10.95 • Paper • ISBN 0-89594-789-7

Changing the World One Relationship at a Time: *Focused listening for Mutual Support and Empowerment*

By Sheryl Karas

Could you use some support so that you can go after the life of your dreams? Changing the World One Relationship at a Time will provide you with the information, skills, and practice you need to arrive at a more joyous life.

$10.95 • Paper • ISBN 0-89594-945-8

Growing Old Disgracefully

By The Hen Co-op

"Every woman approaching sixty, whether alone or still in a relationship, should read this book. It is not only full of good ideas, it's a very good read."—*Sunday News*, Belfast

$12.95 • Paper • ISBN 0-89594-672-6

No More Frogs, No More Princes: *Women Making Creative Choices in Midlife*

Interviews by Joanne Vickers and Barbara Thomas

This book contains 20 women's stories by typical American women who woke up to the possibilities of midlife creativity and met life head on.

$10.95 • Paper • ISBN 0-89594-625-4